IN A DARKNESS

In
a
Darkness

JAMES A. WECHSLER

with Nancy F. Wechsler and Holly W. Karpf

W · W · NORTON & COMPANY · INC ·

NEW YORK

Copyright © 1972 by James A. Wechsler. All rights reserved. Published simultaneously in Canada by George J. McLeod Limited, Toronto. Printed in the United States of America.

Library of Congress Cataloging in Publication Data
Wechsler, James Arthur, 1915–
      In a darkness.
      1.   Mental illness—Personal narratives.
2.   Wechsler, Michael, 1942-1969.   I.   Title.
RC463.W4   616.89′82′00924 [B]   71-38847
ISBN 0-393-07468-4

1 2 3 4 5 6 7 8 9 0

Contents

5-8 0 9

Author's Note

IT WILL BE APPARENT, I hope, that this book is in the deepest sense a collaboration. For reasons of structural convenience and continuity, it was agreed that I would appear to be the narrator; in fact, Nancy wrote some sections separately and in some cases her words are incorporated without attribution; there are other places where they are explicitly ascribed to her—and where even our differences in the evaluation of some episodes are indicated. Holly participated throughout in the planning and preparation and wrote some of her own remembrances.

Most of all we hope that those of Michael's words contained herein—his prose and poetry alike—make this no less his book than a book about him.

❖   ❖   ❖

We are indebted to Bob Stein who served diligently as editor and friend during the preparation of the book; to Vivian Cadden, for her initial and steadfast encouragement; and to Evan Thomas, whose sympathetic interest and sensitivity contributed so much to the final presentation. The nature of the book will suggest why we warmly acknowledge some of those who did so much to sustain us when love and friendship most keenly mattered—David Karpf, Helene and Osmond Fraenkel, Herbert and Doris Wechsler, Richard Sachs, George and Libby Fraenkel, Joseph Cadden, and others too numerous to list.

In preparing the manuscript we had the invaluable help of Carole Dozier Lee; we are also grateful for the assistance of Eve Berliner, Rena Steinzor, and Carmen Figueroa.

J.A.W.

IN A DARKNESS

I

"A Patient Heroism"

IN A SENSE this is both preface and prologue.

This book could hardly have been written as a contrived suspense story. To those who cared, it is no secret that Michael ended his life sometime in the early hours of May 16, 1969, at the age of twenty-six, by consuming an overdose of death-dealing barbiturates. To those who knew nothing about him but live in the shadow of a comparable agony, what may be of value in this remembrance is some relevance to their own perplexity and sadness.

It cannot be called his life story, because there are too many things we do not know and much we may never understand. Yet neither would it have been tolerable to present it solely as a clinical case history. What rendered Michael both so precious and tragic a figure was that, even during most of the worst hours of his private torment, he did not become a nonperson. Until the end, he was alternately fighting to retain or regain an identity that has grown more distinct and imperishable in memory.

If this were to be only a testament, or a love letter mailed too late, it would have been proper to write it only for private circulation. But it must begin on that note. For above all, as we ponder those long years—almost a decade—in which Michael fought the elusive demons of "mental illness," what stands out is our underestimation of how brave and lonely that effort was.

Amid the many letters we received after Michael's death, we especially valued one because it said what we hope this book will indicate about both the grace of his spirit and the valor of his struggle:

I do not know what to say except that we are sure that all those years were not wasted and that all your love was not useless. Beverly was saying Monday, after we had heard, what incredible respect we ought to have for kids like Mike who fought so hard under such a load for so long. We can, I think, remember a patient heroism in such lives that ought to make us prouder of them than we could be of any child who had an easy way to go.

What I shall remember about Mike was not this sadness but how sweet and gentle he was.

We haven't anything else to send you both but our love.

Affectionately, Murray [Kempton]

When a plaque was placed in the new Fieldston School Library in Michael's memory, my brother, Herbert Wechsler, wrote in similar vein:

You dedicate to Michael's memory a corner of a library, where youngsters in the years to come may wage the battle of the mind for understanding of themselves and of the world. It is the right memorial for one whose struggle was so poignant for so long. As we recall the bright and gentle personality we loved, let us remember also that accepting nature's limitations is not surrender but the strongest test of courage.

And there was this letter from a friend of Michael's whom we have never met:

I have learned only recently of Michael's death and wish to extend my sorrow and consolation to you.

I lived next to him my last year at Harvard and we enjoyed many bicycle trips together, as well as sharing the seemingly endless discussions that are the prerogative of undergraduates. I later visited him a few times in the Village and only then began to realize the depth of his despair.

I was a medical student at —— when he was hospitalized there, but, despite repeated attempts, was never permitted to visit him. On one occasion I left him my copy of Yeats.

Despite his unhappiness, Michael was for me a stimulating, understanding, loyal and compassionate friend.

George Stewart, M.D.

Each of these messages was saying what it seems most important to say at the start. We know that Michael's death will shadow all our remaining hours on earth—and we will never cease to ask ourselves questions about whether it could have been prevented, at least at that time and place, and whether a reprieve might have produced new opportunities for recovery. But the stirring memory is the quality of his tenacious battle for life and his confrontation with death. A wise man has said, "It is not death men fear but dying." For Michael, who had contemplated self-destruction so often, we should like to believe that his final act was the triumph of courage after an interminable soliloquy. We grieve that the end was joyless. It is not, however, for those who were spared his trial to judge his choice but rather to cry out against the ignorance and ineptitude still afflicting our exploration of the inscrutable malignancies of the mind.

Yet to have written this only as a form of tribute would be, as I have said, a very private act. Of course, in part it was begun to resist the intolerable truth that Michael is dead, and that there would be no record of his life beyond the bleak obituary notices, which could recite no worldly achievement or characterize any special presence. But as we pressed more deeply into the past, and as we heard from so many after his death, there was a deepening conviction that some of what will be recounted here could have meaning for others.

One reaction to Michael's suicide almost immediately reinforced that point. Not long after he had been pronounced dead —"for several hours," as the doctor at Roosevelt Hospital put it —the police immediately volunteered to suppress the circumstances in which they had found him after responding to our emergency call. And a sensitive *New York Times* reporter who telephoned apologetically swiftly indicated that he would not press us for the crucial details if we preferred to remain silent.

The implication in much of this was that it would involve some humiliation for us to admit that Michael had taken his own life, and that his brief span on earth should not be "tarnished" by the disclosure that death was self-inflicted. Even in the numbness of those hours we were astonished at the prevalence of the view that suicide was a dishonorable or at least disreputable matter, to be charitably covered up to protect Michael's good name and the sensibilities of his family.

Soon after Michael's death we agreed to publish a brief reminiscence in a *New York Post* column. Shortly thereafter we

received a letter from Mrs. Burton Joseph, president of the Na-
tional Association for Mental Health, in which she wrote:

By telling the story of your son's mental illness, of his tortured
years which you and all who loved him could not penetrate, you have
done a great service to millions of Michaels in the world. Only when
there is an awareness, acceptance and understanding of the existence
of mental illness; only when we all face the fact without fear, only
when we can erase the stigma; only when we know that it can happen to any one of us and to those we love; only then can an informed
and unafraid people face the number one health problem in the world
today.

We should have been less surprised by the prevalence of the
taboos. We had observed during Michael's illness the discomfort
he often suffered from being identified as a "mental patient" and
had sensed how being set apart this way had complicated his
problems in those moments when he began to glimpse even fleet-
ingly some faint hope in his long night. I do not believe we ever
quite succeeded in convincing Michael that we recognized his
"patient heroism" (perhaps partly because we succumbed too
often to the counsel of some therapists who equated any such
expression with "coddling" and who intermittently reproached
us for failing to take a sufficiently hard line with him).

Indeed, if there is a single message in these pages, it is that
those who see in Michael some resemblance to someone they
love resist being intimidated by professional counsel and place
some faith in their own instincts. This is not to derogate the
need for such counsel—too many are denied it for lack of private means or public resources—but, rather, to warn that it may
often be conflicting, confusing, and stifling.

Before Michael's death and perhaps to a greater degree afterward, we tried to learn more about the nature of his night-
mare but we have not been graced by any belated revelation.
We have grappled more and more with the question of whether
the illness—ultimately to be diagnosed as schizophrenia—from
which Michael suffered had chemical or organic derivation, and
whether that explains why so much conventional therapy, especially in the last months, was essentially worthless or even
harmful. This may well be the decisive realm of research in the
coming years. Yet we cannot comfortably assume that the out-

come was foreordained and that what we might have said and done differently along the way might not have mattered.

There were discernible peaks and valleys in Michael's life, perhaps only more extreme than those that others find to be a bearable—"normal"—state of flux. An eminent criminologist has said that the line between "sanity and insanity" is the most wavering, imprecise demarcation in all human affairs, and who can surely isolate the elements that tip the fragile balance?

We have called this book *In a Darkness* because that is how we felt during so many of the years when Michael was in the hands of a long procession of therapists, and when, except for rare interludes, we were excluded from the treatment rooms. We look back now and see too many moments when we were awed by psychiatric dogma that too often proved irrelevant or inconsistent. At times, Nancy and I differed in our own evaluations. Yet there were clearly hours along the way to which we wish we could return, most of all in the last weeks when a signal we were given was misinterpreted and minimized by the therapist then in charge, and we failed to pursue it. The circumstance will be described in detail because it may offer some clues to others who are failing to hear or heed a warning.

This may indicate that we have undertaken an inquest, but that is not our intention. We have never even attempted to find out how Michael amassed the pills he used on the last night. Presumably he would have found them once he had resolved to do so, and whatever negligence may have been involved—whether that of a pharmacist, therapist, or ourselves—could not have been crucial. Or at least so we concluded.

Neither have we tried to interrogate Michael's numerous therapists. Of all of them we can say quite confidently that their devotion to him never seemed in doubt. Certainly none was in desperate need of patients; in fact, all were flourishing practitioners on one level or another and, in some instances, gave Michael a measure of attention and concern that transcended the fifty-minute ritual. What we might learn from them now would create hopeless complexity in trying to determine which comments were self-serving and trying to reconcile contradictory appraisals which so often enhanced our own confusion while he was alive.

So, in deciding instead to set down the way things appeared from the misty distance through which we frequently saw them, the result may be that we have written more about ourselves than about Michael, which he might have seen as the final affront. We have tried to give some portrait of him, and of the music he imparted to so many whose lives he touched, and some glimpses of the unfulfilled talents and sense of beauty reflected in the unfinished poetry of his life, which we found stored away in his desk. What we have to offer are only fragments, and we know that any overstatement would have offended him.

"Do not feel guilty," wrote a friend whose husband had destroyed himself after convincing the doctors at the hospital where he had been under treatment that it was entirely safe for him to go home. But, of course, there can never be any refuge for those who were unable to speak the words that might somehow have made life endurable for a little while longer (for who knows what might have happened thereafter?) to one they loved.

During his long battle, Michael was treated for varying intervals by eight therapists over a period of nine years, as well as by innumerable interns whom he encountered during periods of hospitalization that began in 1964. The therapists are identified by number, rather than name, in the order of their initial appearance. He spent more than twenty-six months in five institutions, which will be assigned fictitious names—Pleasant View, Fairhope, Statewide, Brightlawn, and Grace Hills. It was in one of those hospitals that he wrote these lines:

> It's a feeling of hopelessness, creeping, casual but sure,
> How much more, Dr. Freud, can I endure?

His deepening sense of futility about the varieties of therapy to which he had been exposed was recorded in his notebook two months before his death:

> There is an earthly paradise
>   in my mind, which I cannot find . . .
> Must I wait for chemical coincidence in my brain,
> Will they, as they have before, just drive me insane?

Why did he finally conclude that he was doomed? Why, after all the years in which he had groped for daylight and mo-

mentarily glimpsed it along the way, was there no one from
whom he could derive any further confidence?

We hope this will not be read either as an exercise in self-
critical recall or futile recrimination, but elements of both are
probably inevitable. Ours has often been a hectic, turbulent
home, affected by the public tensions in which we lived, by
chemical differences between ourselves, and by the intermittent
stresses that afflict almost any marriage of long duration. (We
were both under nineteen when we were married at college; Michael was born eight years later.) Psychiatrists who insist that
their patients choose parents for whom life has been a never-
never land of tranquillity would be conspicuously underem-
ployed.

It is unlikely that even such warm, thoughtful friends as Bob
Stein and Vivian Cadden would have urged us to set down
these remembrances if Michael's death had not signified something about the unease of our times. By this we do not mean the
apocalyptic state of the world, although these are not wholly
unrelated matters. Many sought in conveying their sympathy to
us to depict Michael as a victim of the atomic age and of the
eternity of the Vietnam war, and this would be an easy pretext
both for outrage and for reconciliation to the outcome.

The reality, however, is that Michael's death climaxed nearly
ten years of illness that began, or became manifest, just before
the beginning of the bright, brief Kennedy era. It spared him
any risk of conscription during the Vietnam conflict. (Once,
when he was protesting his prolonged sickness and I offered the
poor comfort that he was at least facing no immediacy of being
entrapped in the war, he exclaimed angrily, "That might be better than the way I'm living." On another occasion, he was to
say, "I wish I could wake up feeling really bad—it would be
better than feeling nothing.")

There is no way of measuring how Michael's anxieties were
aggravated by the pressures of a violent time. He was eleven
years old when I was called before the McCarthy investigating
committee. Through much of his childhood and youth he must
have been awakened often by the sound of a phone ringing in
the middle of the night, heralding some journalistic or world crisis. Perhaps we knew too little of the insecurities intensified by
such turmoil, and the degree to which they shaped the drug cul-

ture in which Michael was eventually to become involved. But
many others have survived, and we would be deluding ourselves
if we simplistically traced suicide to society and discounted his
own illness.

His farewell note, gentle and muted, spoke for itself:

> Sorry, but one can't keep every promise. Don't blame yourselves,
> or anyone. Please don't let it hurt you. You must be together, and go
> on with each other.
>
> Mike

That he left this note was an ultimate compassion; at least it
dispelled any mystery as to what had happened and the deliber-
ateness of the act. It imparted to what might otherwise have
seemed a momentary aberration or a ghastly accident a tone of
reflection and resolution.

Now we can only try to retrace the long, lonely road he
walked before those last words were written and hope others
will find some new light along the way.

II

Dr. First

WHERE DOES HISTORY begin when what is being written is neither biography nor case study but rather a retrospect that may faintly illuminate a darkness?

To say, without Michael's testimony, that one moment was crucial is a presumption. As I began to write this passage, I recalled a day at least two years before any therapy began, a time when he was still so much the "normal boy" at the Fieldston School; Michael had just come home from a dance for high school students on the Columbia campus. He had told Nancy with some embarrassment that, as he stepped into the street off the island in the middle of 116th Street, he had failed to glance at the oncoming traffic and been brushed by a passing vehicle. He had also asked her not to tell me of the episode because, he said, he feared I would have undue concern.

He was about fifteen at the time. Why had he seen so much significance in the episode? Was he already trying to say something that we had not even dimly glimpsed? It did not occur to us—in view of his admonition to Nancy—to pursue the question, or, alas, even to wonder much about it.

Now it is the spring of 1960 and, in early afternoon, Michael, who is seventeen and a senior in high school, has telephoned me at my office. His initial words, perhaps because I was to repeat them so often in reciting the chronology to so many doctors, are unforgettably clear:

"Dad, would you mind doing me an expensive favor?

My answer was, "Well, tell me what it is," probably in a tone of acquiescence.

He said, "I'd like to see a psychiatrist."

I said that, of course, that would be all right and I would try to come home early to talk to him about it.

He said, "No, I'd like to do it right away." He explained that his closest friend had been under treatment by Dr. First for some time. Michael had already talked to Dr. First, who had told him he would see him that afternoon if I sanctioned the visit. I demurred momentarily but weakly. There came to mind a sudden image of Michael sitting on a window ledge, and some desperate risk of delay. I yielded without any extensive debate. It was not difficult to do so; it offered quick relief from anxiety, perhaps even a self-indulgence.

It seemed obvious that the next step would be for us to meet Dr. First and, after talking briefly with Michael that evening, I called him, assuming that we would promptly arrange an appointment. And thus began a nine-year misunderstanding—I can really think of no more precise or generous word—in which Michael was often to feel himself an embattled bystander.

To what I thought was an almost routine request for an appointment, Dr. First replied that it was not his custom to meet with parents during the first stage of treatment. Later we learned that this was a position adopted by many in his profession. But, if my own sense of disaster can be traced to any single occasion, it is to that phone call. Dr. First could hardly have failed to be aware of my angry reaction and of the grudging fashion in which I finally assented to his terms.

After we had approached the brink of a break-off in the conversation, and I had reluctantly drawn back, he observed that Michael was a "very sick" boy. Apart from his psychological distress, Dr. First said, Michael was suffering from "rectal bleeding."

This physiological detail was to become one of the sources of much mystifying diversionary trouble. That Dr. First employed it is simply beyond dispute; Nancy, who was seated about twenty feet away in the living room while I talked to him, remembers that I referred to it almost immediately and, in the ensuing gloom, we agreed that the first thing to do was to have Michael examined by our family pediatrician. We saw him a few days later, and when I mentioned the matter of "rectal bleeding," he said this was fairly commonplace among young men and often signified brief, transitory homosexual experiences.

However, when he examined Michael soon thereafter, he found no evidence of such a condition or of any other physical problem.

Subsequently, Michael was to contend on many occasions that Dr. First had assured him that he had never given me any such report and to charge that I had invented the story. This, of course, I know I had not done. I still grope for explanations that might justify the thought that there had been some misunderstanding of so explicit a remark. If I had not relayed the report so swiftly to Nancy and we had not acted on it so promptly, I might be tempted to believe that I really had been the victim of a delusion, or a faulty connection. But of all the ambiguously ominous things Dr. Frist said that night, the words *rectal bleeding* remain unmistakably clear. Perhaps Dr. First's later disclaimers were inherent in the protective relationship that grew out of his treatment of Michael, and the adversary tension between father and son that was to be expected—so a number of psychiatrists were to tell me—in the course of therapy. I can no longer hope to discover whether, for reasons that still elude me, I had been told a lie, a half-truth, or a fact that was beyond medical detection by the time of the pediatrician's examination.

All that now seems clear—as it did so often thereafter—is that it was hopeless to try, as I believe both Dr. First and I intermittently did, to overcome the animosity with which our relationship began.

After about two weeks, Dr. First consented to see Nancy and me. There were two or three sessions during that spring, sometimes with all three of us present, at least once in separate audiences. It is no longer possible to isolate the conversations and relate them sequentially.

But the shattering news—or verdict—was rendered by Dr. First in our first meeting. He told us that Michael would require treatment for a considerable time—perhaps as long as seven years, and possibly (or did he say probably?) recurrent treatment for the rest of his life. He offered no quickly comprehensible diagnosis (*schizophrenia, manic-depressive,* and other terms that began to sound interchangeable were to come much later, from many therapists). The most tangible description he gave of

Michael's condition was that he suffered from "obsessive thoughts" dealing, for example, with recurrent images of feces. Revealing my own illiteracy in this realm, I volunteered the information that I, too, had "obsessions," chiefly relating to fantasies about athletic events, and often achieved sleep by playing out various games in my head. Dr. First made it clear rather curtly that the analogy was crude and ignorant, as, of course, it essentially was.

This first personal encounter was painfully unsuccessful. It should be said at this point that neither Nancy nor I had any instinctive or doctrinaire animus toward psychiatry. If anything, the reverse was true. Quite early in her life we had felt that our daughter Holly's anxieties were serious enough to warrant psychiatric scrutiny, and we had taken her to Dr. Edward Liss, a long-time friend of Nancy's family. Dr. Liss, a warm, generous, undogmatic spirit, had immeasurably fortified Holly, as she was to attest many times. Indeed, one of the ghastly paradoxes is that during the period of Holly's early stress that seriously obstructed her attendance at school Michael seemed a felicitously balanced, poised, and considerate older brother.

In any other kind of illness, it would have seemed routine for us to take Michael to Dr. Liss for treatment, and it is hard to believe that there would have been any tug of war about the decision. But because Dr. Liss had been Holly's therapist, he himself deemed it unwise to take charge of the case; he was willing only to serve as our consultant and did so generously until his death early in 1967.

We might also have been disposed to urge Michael to turn to Dr. R., who was to come to our help at a critical juncture much later; he was a friend of ours from our college years and a man for whom we had great esteem and affection. But Michael knew his daughters socially and we assumed this would be a major obstacle. In fact, when we directly asked him at a later stage to become Michael's therapist, Dr. R. confirmed that judgment and reluctantly declined to do so.

Yet it was partially because of our warm relationship with Dr. Liss, which had already proved so rewarding by the time we became aware of Michael's illness, that I found this initial confrontation (the use of the word is perhaps self-revealing) so depressing. Nancy's first reaction was certainly less negative than mine at the time; for many months, she actually became a kind of mediator between us, and her subsequent disenchantment is, therefore, perhaps more consequential. Indeed, Nancy's recollections about the first meetings suggest how ambiguous her reactions were:

I remember Dr. First indicating a long period of therapy ahead, but I have no recollection that he—or anyone in the early years—ever suggested that the illness would get worse, or, indeed, that it was mental illness as distinguished from neurosis requiring psychiatric help. No doctor in the four years before the first breakdown and hospitalization ever even hinted that the problem would acquire such dimensions. Perhaps I was simply being obtuse. But I had known many people who had had extensive therapy, and who lived with serious but manageable neuroses, so the idea of a long period of *treatment*, in light of the kind of boy Michael had been, did not lead me to expect psychotic breakdown and hospitalization. We knew a man who was unable to go underground, a woman who couldn't go higher than the second floor, grown women who could not move away from their city of birth because they could not leave their mothers, and so on. But they managed to live in society. It was this sort of prospect, a dependence on psychiatrists and a degree of crippling from neurosis, that I associated with such early prognosis as we got—never insanity.

No doctor—including Liss—ever prepared us for what happened. What Liss did, in the first year, was to confirm that there was a real problem—until then we were not sure whether there was or not. After Michael was given a Rorschach test (which Dr. First suggested and then, after Liss agreed, said was unnecessary), I was convinced, because Liss was convinced, that Mike did need systematic treatment. I thought it was for the "obsessive" problems and that, in time, they would be resolved, although I accepted the idea that Mike might have some handicaps.

At first I was even more incredulous than Nancy that a prognosis of extended therapy could be presented with such certitude. We were to find out later that Dr. First had known Michael for several months before taking him as his patient. It seems that Michael had gone along on several of his friend's visits to Dr. First and had become acquainted with him. In any event, Dr. First was not talking about a stranger when he assessed the gravity of Michael's problems and the long therapeutic journey he faced.

But then, as for so many times thereafter and to this moment, I have wondered whether such pronouncement of a kind of indeterminate sentence contains elements of self-fulfilling prophecy.

While Michael had been unusually tense and withdrawn in the days before the telephone call about the appointment with Dr. First, there had been no overt indication of serious trouble. On the evening before Michael's phone call, I remember remarking to him that he seemed quite "down" and asking him with what must have seemed stereotyped casualness, "Having trouble about a girl?" He glared at me angrily, and then he left the room.

In view of what Dr. First said, we dared not stop the treatment; yet we knew nothing about First or his credentials. We consulted Dr. Liss, who did not know First but, after inquiry, observed that his qualifications were acceptable. We talked with others in the field, with similar results. We arranged for Michael to be examined by his pediatrician and to see Dr. Liss. Then Dr. Liss talked to Dr. First. Neither Liss nor the pediatrician doubted that Michael should receive psychiatric treatment, and, as things stood, the only open question was whether to insist on a different therapist. But the reports on Dr. First gave us no basis for questioning his professional standing.

Since Michael made it plain that he was determined to be treated by Dr. First, the premonitions of family stress were already in the air. But there did not seem to be any valid reason for disputing Michael's choice of his psychiatrist.

It must be reiterated—if only because others may find themselves in the same setting—that neither Nancy nor I fully grasped, as we see it now, the gravity of Dr. First's announcement. I suppose I had written as many editorials as anyone else about The Problem of Mental Illness, and the need for more adequate subsidization of treatment, and so forth. Yet I was slow to acknowledge what was to become the reality of the long subsequent years.

In part this was due to the fact that other doctors who succeeded Dr. First either did not share his morose prediction or perhaps preferred not to echo it in our presence. The obvious question is whether Dr. First was more prescient than some of the others, or whether the forecast—of which Michael must have been aware, although we never explicitly discussed it— had any bearing on the recurrence of breakdowns, the loss of confidence, and his final despair.

From early spring until Michael entered college in the fall, he saw Dr. First regularly (except while Nancy, Holly, and he were on a six-week cross-country driving trip). During the spring he was anxious and uncommunicative; otherwise there were few outward changes. He went about his business at high school and his work there seemed unaffected. But Nancy recalls one unusual episode that foreshadowed the future. One after- noon Michael came home and demanded that Nancy immedi- ately give him twenty dollars to buy records. He had no good reason for the demand, but he insisted vehemently that he felt a desperate need to go downtown to buy them at once. Nancy's instinct was to say no. But since such bizarre behavior was wholly uncharacteristic, she called Dr. First, who said, "Don't you realize, Mrs. Wechsler, that he is saying to you, 'Mother, I'm sick?' " and advised that Michael be given the twenty dol- lars.

There were no comparable episodes until much later, but during that spring and summer there was growing tension be- tween Michael and me about Dr. First, and the conflict about the course of Michael's treatment steadily increased.

With Michael approaching graduation from Fieldston and scheduled to enter college in the autumn, there was the immedi- ate problem of whether he should feel free to leave the city. Be- fore the disclosure of his need for treatment, he had applied to Harvard, Columbia, and Chicago; all accepted him, but his preference was unmistakably Harvard. (That was not only the prestige choice of most of Michael's generation; it was where Nancy's father and brother had gone, and the only college Mi- chael had been willing to visit.) There were unspoken but, we believed, deep-seated reasons why Michael was reluctant to at- tend Columbia. Twenty-five years earlier I had gone there and some echoes of my participation in the undergraduate rebellion of that time had been heard in the McCarthy hearings. A desire for an independent identity is scarcely unique in influencing a young man's choice of college. It may be that we exaggerated the problem or simply read it into Michael's desire for Harvard. But it certainly inhibited us from questioning whether it was wise for Michael to head for Cambridge at that time, especially since Dr. First strongly backed his decision.

While emphasizing the depth and possible duration of Michael's troubles, Dr. First was no less certain that he could meet the trials of existence at Harvard. He even expressed confidence that it would not be necessary to obtain supplementary treatment in Cambridge or even communicate with the Harvard Health Service. It was Dr. First's belief that, by seeing Michael during holiday trips to New York he could provide the requisite aid.

We were uneasy about the decision. But we had already begun the process of suppressing doubt and yielding to counsel in a realm in which our naïveté was still mixed with some measure of disbelief about the magnitude of the ailment. At Fieldston's commencement Michael appeared quiet, reserved, poised, if at moments uneasy, but there is always an underlying nervousness at such exercises. In our eyes, he seemed conspicuously handsome and well groomed. On that rather humid but sunlit day, when Michael joined with his classmates in their commencement rituals on Fieldston's tranquil lawn, his appearance and demeanor seemed to confound the portrait of a "very sick boy" and to revive our illusion that he would quickly overcome any transitory disturbance.

III

The Years of Sunlight

IN AN ANGRY MOMENT, Michael once exclaimed, "You know, Dad, I wasn't *born* this way."

The accusation required no elaboration. He was saying what he—and others—were later to say in one way or another in many family therapy sessions we attended: that their illness could be traced to some parental failure or neglect.

From all the evidence of outward behavior, Michael had not been "born that way." From earliest childhood, one associated with him the music of laughter, a certain mastery of spontaneous social relationships and mechanical complexity, a quiet courtesy and diffidence.

On my office desk, since the time when our family returned from Washington to New York in 1949, there had been a picture of Michael and Holly, probably taken about a year earlier when he was six and she was two. They are sitting on the small terrace outside our Georgetown home. Michael, in a white sweatshirt, is grinning—almost mugging—with one eye half closed in a whimsical wink; Holly is standing beside him a little anxiously, and her face is quite solemn.

In the ensuing eleven years, to the time of that phone call from Michael asking to see a psychiatrist, there was no working day when I did not see that picture and take some pleasure in Michael's wonderfully captivating smile. During those years they would visit my office together, and *Post* photographer Tony Calvacca, who was to encourage Michael's interest in his craft, delighted in taking pictures of them. One of the last, showing them walking together, must have been made when Michael was about fifteen and Holly eleven; again Michael exhibited a rather serene gaiety and Holly a certain reserve. Together they were a lovely sight, with Holly now confident and gracious and Mi-

chael, as we had known him for so long, seemingly relaxed, un-
troubled, and endowed with so many varied skills.

Michael's sudden request to see a psychiatrist was at once
stunning and implausible. Almost from infancy he had seemed
so capable of coping with life, so full of zest and self-assurance,
so endowed with characteristics that others might identify as
those of "a happy child" and later "a model boy."

Early in Michael's life, Nancy recalls reading Gesell's book
on how children behave at various ages. She found that his activities were almost entirely usual, except that he sometimes
seemed about six months ahead of himself. Such precocity, however gratifying, in no way altered the basic impression of almost
uncanny normality, such as Gesell's notation that small boys at
a particular age reveled in playing with strings, which was exactly what Michael, to our puzzlement (until Gesell), had been
doing.

These are some of Nancy's other notes about those early
years:

"When Mike was about ten months old he would awaken
very early. I would get him up, put him in his playpen, and go
back to bed. If he wanted something he couldn't reach, he
would stick his foot out through the slots and push the playpen
around, as if punting a boat.

"After Holly was born, her crib was kept in his bedroom at
night (we lived at the time in a one-bedroom apartment). Mike
objected to 'that baby' crying and keeping him awake, so we
moved 'that baby' into the living room (which was our bedroom) at night. Mike also said around then that he wondered
when we were going to give 'that baby' back. Later, when Holly
was still a baby, Mike paid little attention to her. He went to
school by then, and after we moved to a house of our own, he
had friends on the block with whom he was occupied much of
the time. There was a back yard in which he dug large holes.
He had a three-wheel bike that he rode around the block, making friends with people along the way. He became especially
friendly with the people who ran the candy store on the corner.

"The first time I took him to be interviewed by a nursery
school, it was a school in process of organization, and we were
interviewed by the principal of the school (who was not himself

a teacher). There was an old player piano in the schoolroom. Mike, always fascinated by mechanical things, asked the principal how the player piano worked. The principal said he didn't know and gave Mike a piece of paper and suggested that he draw something on it. Mike rejected the paper, asking the principal how he could be a teacher if he didn't know how the piano worked.

"When he was about eighteen months old, we took him visiting one Sunday in the country, and after lunch we put him to bed in someone else's crib. Soon afterward he was found, dressed only in diapers, behind the wheel of a parked car, playing at steering.

"When Michael was four or five he occasionally walked in his sleep, and he began making a fuss about going to sleep, demanding one thing after another at bedtime. The pediatrician finally suggested that we just tell him to go to sleep and let him yell if necessary. One night's adherence to that prescription ended the cycle.

"When he was about seven, I was stricken with mononucleosis and we had no maid. Michael made breakfast for the family in the morning.

"He was a physically active little boy—he walked early; he learned to climb out of his crib almost as soon as he could walk. He was the kind of boy who makes a dash for what interests him and gets right into it. He talked late and showed little interest in books or sedentary games. When he was about four, he went to summer nursery school with a friend of his age who was timid and shy. Mike took him by the hand and took care of him until he became used to school. He adapted quickly when he started regular school. He always had friends in the neighborhood and at school. He was very definite about what he wanted to do, and he didn't give up easily. He had good coordination and learned to play games and swim easily. When we left Washington, his schoolteacher there told me that Mike had been a great 'jokemaker' in the first grade and had kept the class amused.

"After we moved, he went to the local public school, which was considered a good school, although quite lacking in nonacademic subject matter. Mike began to paint when he was about seven; he showed rather remarkable talent, and his paternal grandfather encouraged him to paint with oils. (Sometimes when he was unable to accomplish what he was trying to do, he would lose his temper, and I would have to stop the painting until he calmed down.)

"Although he would explode occasionally at his sister, his childhood was not characterized by tantrums. He liked to play active outdoor games; when he was with his more sedate and intellectual cousins he wanted more activity, less talk. On the whole he was gregarious and friendly; he received an honorable citation from a Boy Scout troop.

"He usually had one hobby or interest that absorbed him— one after the other. When a new one started, he abandoned the previous one. After painting, it was playing the piano, then, experimenting with chemistry and radio sets, then photography. He became an excellent photographer, also proficient at developing and enlarging. He often went to Jimmy's office and worked in the darkroom there, and he was friendly with the photographers on the paper. By the time he was in high school the photography began to taper off. He went in for rock and roll; then he turned to classical records. Later he grew interested in model rockets and joined a club at school. I can see now that the rocket-building became a real obsession; he was intent on finding a place where the rockets would be fired. There were no available places, but Mike was quite unreasonable about his continued efforts to persuade us that he had found one. By that time he was about fifteen.

"Summers were spent in Westport, Connecticut, where Mike had a group of friends who, as he did, stayed in Westport rather than going to camp. There was a lot to do there for boys and girls of ten to thirteen, a good deal of freedom of movement, and it seemed a good way for city kids to spend summers. They could bicycle, swim, play ball, and roam around pretty much on their own. As Mike grew older he was anxious to have a driver's license, and he seemed to learn to drive by osmosis; he needed no elaborate instruction. He was the member of the family we all relied on to fix or build whatever was needed.

"Mike seemed to become interested in girls around the time he was eleven or twelve, but his attachments came and went swiftly. Later, at about fourteen, he went to school dances and to parties, but he had no steady girl and did very little regular dating when he was in high school.

"We sent Mike to private school starting in the fourth grade. Most of the children were well off, surrounded by possessions. Mike did well in school, but in the early years there was nothing outstanding about his school record. It was later, in high school, that his schoolwork began to be notable. There were always some 'problem' children in his class, or children who needed some kind of special attention. Mike was considered one of the reliable 'good citizens' who cooperated, did his work, was a 'good sport' in athletics. By high school, although the faculty had no complaints about him, Mike began, along with a group of friends, to withdraw from the social mainstream of the class and look with some disdain at the conventional social activities. But there was nothing very dramatic about this disaffection.

"He was a reliable student and equally conscientious at home. He got where he was supposed to be on time, he helped when he was asked to help. Mike got along more easily at school than Holly did. He was well coordinated and good at games; Holly clearly disliked competitive sports. Sometimes Mike was impatient with Holly; sometimes he exploded when she did. Sometimes he was helpful and protective; much of the time he was busy with his own friends, his schoolwork, and his hobbies. When they were growing up, until Mike was well along in the illness, it seemed evident that he was older, stronger, and the leader in most situations where both were involved. (As the illness intensified, their roles became reversed. Mike was the one more likely to have childish tantrums and be in need of protection in social situations. It was Holly who tried gallantly to find friends for him and to give him support.)

"He had a real sense of color and form from an early age. The painting he did as early as seven showed a fine color sense, and the photography he did later showed form and balance. Much of his photography was concentrated on people—his sister, his grandparents, the maid, and his friends; and he took the camera along on school trips and events. Our cabinets are crowded with those pictures—many personal portraits, pictures of a fire in the neighborhood, a Macy's Thanksgiving parade, springtime scenes of the boat basin in the park, the house in Westport. One day, when we were riding the subway uptown, I told Mike that the man sitting across the way was former Mayor Vincent Impellitteri. Mike 'stole' a candid picture, and the next day it appeared in the news section of the *Post:* 'Photo by Mike Wechsler.'

"He always wanted the best equipment for his current hobby, and he wanted it right away. He was unhappy about waiting until Christmas or a birthday, but most of the time he had to wait. Although he could be very insistent about the kind of camera or enlarger he thought he should have, he was usually reasonable about compromise. However, the preoccupation with things was recurrent. For instance, he didn't just want a watch, he wanted an antimagnetic waterproof watch. Since most of his classmates had even more expensive possessions, I was never sure whether such desires reflected something special about Mike, or simply the school environment.

"I think now that Michael felt under a special compulsion to live up to a standard of being a good boy when he was small, perhaps because Holly was having problems of adjustment. So when the car had to be loaded for the journey to the country, he was the one to help; when Jimmy's parents took over as baby-sitters and had trouble persuading Holly to behave, they expected Mike to be good and to help them, and he was and he did. Years later, after he had become ill, Mike once said that Holly had always been better at expressing herself than he, and I wondered how much he had been suppressing over the years in which he was being helpful, responsible, and cooperative.

"From the earliest years he was infatuated with autos. When he was sixteen, he spent hours driving around Connecticut looking for a car for my parents and ultimately found one. He was a talented bargain hunter and negotiator. He was quite scornful of his parents' disinclination to bargain.

"Mike was almost always willing to go to school, but otherwise he resisted being organized. When he was about six, he took piano lessons. He loved the teacher, played a lot, did a lot of improvising. The teacher left, and when he found the new one unsympathetic and authoritarian, he asked not to have any more lessons. That was the end of his career at the piano.

"Years later, in college, he took up the guitar, then, in the hospital after a serious motorcycle accident, he took up the flute, and from then on the flute and the recorder were important in his life. Before he left Harvard he had begun to concentrate a good deal on the flute. But he never wanted to engage in organized musical activity; when he was older he collected records and divulged a keen interest in classical music, but he had no particular interest in going to concerts.

"He was apparently more articulate with his friends than at home. I remember being startled when Mike was fifteen and a friend whose daughter Mike visited a good deal in Westport remarked on how surprised he was that his daughter was interested in an 'intellectual like Mike.' I often thought that Mike would ultimately make a career in art, music, or something like architecture. However, as he grew older, he seemed to feel the need to pursue an intellectual career. Characteristically, when he went to Harvard, he refused to take easy courses and insisted on a demanding schedule with heavy reading requirements.

"I remember one evening in the summer in Westport when Mike was about sixteen. He and his friends did a lot of driving around in the evening, and this evening he was getting ready to go out on a date, talking to another boy as he combed his hair. He was talking about how unreasonable someone else had been in a social situation and about how best to cool things. His voice was level and calm; he seemed quite mature, in charge of himself, the solid citizen to whom others looked for guidance."

To Nancy's recollections, Holly adds these:
"As a small child my view of my older brother was mingled with awe and irritation. On the one hand, he treated me as the annoying pest, which I suppose that I was. We had the usual spats and disagreements, but my overall impression was that my brother was someone very special, someone to be idealized. I proudly displayed his picture to my girl friends at school and reveled in their admiration of his good looks. Michael was very successful academically and painstakingly helped me with my schoolwork, particularly mathematics and science. When I was in seventh grade, he helped me build a transistor radio for my science class.

"I remember the day the acceptance from Harvard came. I was in eighth grade at the time and Michael had just begun to treat me as a person, confiding in me just a little. We both arrived home together and saw the letter waiting for him. His face broke into a broad smile as he said, 'Since it begins with "It is our pleasure to inform you," I guess it's good.' My immediate reaction, after appropriate outbursts of pride, was that I wanted to call my best girl friend. Michael, a bit ironically, requested that he be permitted to make the first call.

"Until the spring of 1964, when Michael began to say that he did not 'feel well enough' to finish his senior year, I had no inkling that he was having emotional problems. I had already decided to major in psychology when I entered college in the fall, not because I wanted to 'help Michael' but because my star of a brother had majored in the subject and I wanted to follow in his footsteps.

"When Michael was recovering from his motorcycle accident, I began taking him with me to parties. At one party, an older friend of mine who had had some emotional problems of his own said to me, 'Watch out for Michael. I can see he's a lot like me.' At the time I thought that this friend didn't know what he was talking about.

"I remember how gentle and helpful Michael was with one of our grandfathers—my father's father—when he was ill. I thought Michael showed a great sensitivity at that time.

"Later, when Michael had been ill for a number of years, he once apologized for not having been very 'nice to me as a child.' I was astounded that Michael felt the need to apologize for what had been his part in a normal and uncomplicated brother-sister rivalry. Yet this seemed to characterize much of Michael's later years—the need to apologize for what he saw as his failures."

There were times in Michael's childhood when the scope and variety of his interests gave me a sense that I could not keep up with him, especially in matters mechanical. But he seemed outwardly satisfied with my admiration for his achievements, even if some were, even when he was quite young, beyond my comprehension or true interest.

The area in which we achieved steadiest companionship was sports but he was, in effect, to outgrow them as I never have. With some sadness, I recall now that our most sustained companionship during his childhood involved games, either playing or watching. Later, I think, he was to be resentful of what he must have regarded as my effort to transform him into the skilled athlete I would like to have been. Perhaps that fantasy did afflict me, but the main problem was that I lacked the imagination or aptitude to discover other things we might have been doing together. I recall, for example, the week when Holly was born and my parents came to stay with Michael and me in Washington. He had his first set of toy trains; due to wartime restrictions on metal it was a rather ramshackle railroad that had to be pieced together. It was my father, with Michael's help (he was then four), who performed the assembly task while I looked on.

But not too many years later I introduced Michael to baseball, and he seemed to share my pleasure in the training. By the time he was about nine we had inserted a very professional home plate into the lawn at Westport. There, sometimes for an hour or more, Michael would pitch to me while I called balls and strikes in a simulated nine-inning game.

As he progressed, I began to hit grounders and flies to him, much in the manner of pregame warm-up at the professional games we had begun to attend together. These seemed to be intervals of mutual fun, although Michael's perfectionism was already triggering small rages. I still recall quite vividly a rather chill, cloud-laden afternoon when I was hitting long flies to him. For some reason he missed a succession of them and grew more furious each time he misjudged the ball or saw it inexplicably bounce out of his glove. Finally I urged that we suspend operations for the day, but he heatedly insisted that we continue until he had caught six or seven consecutively.

There also developed around that time the institution of the father-son weekend softball games. Michael played ably if not brilliantly, but, as the years passed, he grew less competitive and involved. This was also true of some other kids of his age, perhaps because the intensity of some adult participants began to dominate the games. I was one of the fathers who treated them with a solemnity that may have seemed either ludicrous or forbidding to the younger players.

There were other episodes still clear in memory that suggest how my preoccupation with the athletic life, far from establishing a closer association, may have eventually produced more tension and estrangement, or simple bewilderment, than authentic association.

In Michael's sophomore year at Fieldston he and I were in the city together at the start of his semester while Nancy and Holly were still finishing their vacation in Westport. The track coach had persuaded him to try out for the football team because he was persuaded that his speed and agility could make him an outstanding end. At the end of the first week of practice, when we were dining together, Michael said quite apologetically, "I don't think I want to stay with football. I'm sure I'd enjoy playing in the games but all the calisthenics and the rest of the training are very boring."

Obviously he felt that I would be unhappy about his decision. In fact, although I did not say so, I felt rather relieved. Michael was well built and well coordinated, but not really big enough for rugged football competition. Indeed, when he started practice I had grim apprehensions about watching him in actual play. But when I assured him that the decision was entirely his own and that there was no status at stake, I had the uneasy feeling that he nevertheless thought I felt he had somehow failed some test of character. Trying not to say too much, I probably said too little.

Something comparable had occurred during a previous summer when Michael entered a doubles tennis tournament in Westport. His instinctive grace of movement and swiftness of reflex seemed to give him remarkable potential for tennis, discernible in the very early years. But this was the first tournament in which he had participated. The first-round match took place in comparative privacy on a weekday during my August vacation and I sat behind the screen. Michael's partner was one of Westport's mildly celebrated young athletes and together they won the first set quite easily. Then they both began making errors and before too long they found themselves vainly trying to come from behind in the deciding third set. When it was over I had the feeling that Michael's disappointment was very much aggravated by my presence and I rather wished that I had not been there. It was the first and only time that he took part in a tournament.

Yet these episodes may be unworthy of the attention given them here as we try to reconstruct, perhaps too melodramatically, the origins of barriers that were later to become so formidable. My own father was a quiet, gentle man who died in his eighty-ninth year, and our conversations were usually muted and limited, although there was rarely any awkwardness or friction. His concerns, like Michael's, were far less political and more cultural and scientific than mine. I often felt that Michael's wide range of activity and diversion was closer to the interests of my father than to my preoccupation with journalism, politics, and sports.

Michael could not avoid being aware of the intensely political atmosphere in his home, but throughout those years he showed little concern for such matters. Much later, Dr. Third was to tell Nancy that Michael had said he was far less apolitical than we thought, but that he had found it difficult to communicate his interest. I do recall a Sunday when Michael and I were walking in Riverside Park, shortly after I had appeared before the McCarthy investigating committee. The *New York Times* had published a lengthy supportive editorial that week, and Michael remarked rather abruptly, "I hear that you beat Senator McCarthy."

I tried to explain that the outcome of such encounters could not be judged very quickly, and that McCarthy was still very much with us, but that I felt satisfied with the way things had gone. He did not seem disposed to continue the conversation, and I was primarily trying to allay his apprehensions about the notion that I was in any grave trouble. Perhaps I underestimated both his interest and his capacity to absorb what the dispute was about, much of it involving my membership—along with Nancy—in the Young Communist League nearly two decades earlier. In writing a "political autobiography" the following summer, I did suggest that I hoped it would eventually help Michael and Holly understand what the furor had been about.

In any case the storm subsided. Journalistic life continued to be hectic, with too few hours of family quiet and shared excursions. But Michael seemed to be achieving a very full existence of his own and the time we did spend together, if lacking in intimacy of communication, was generally warm and free of strain. Or so I thought.

Moreover, as the Fieldston years went on, there were the constant reassurances contained in both his gregarious social life and the reports from school. In June, 1955, as he finished the seventh grade, the typed report we received about him included these comments, along with grades of good to excellent in every course:

SOCIAL ADJUSTMENT: Michael seems to have spread his friendships and gets along well with both students and adults.

WORK HABITS: Michael has continued in his willingness to try anything and to make the most of suggestions for his own improvement with considerable success. His concentration is excellent in class. He is responsible and serious.

ACHIEVEMENT: Michael has grown considerably in written work, both creative and research. His spelling has improved somewhat along with his handwriting. He has worked for greater accuracy in math and is now working in the upper third of the class. He is also a thoughtful contributor to oral work and has achieved some constructive leadership in classroom activities.

At the end of the eighth grade there, just before his entrance into high school, his report card ranged from excellent to very good.

After he entered high school, the reports were no less gratifying. On November 15, 1957, his scorecard listed him "1"—signifying "commendable achievement"—in all subjects.

On January 30, 1959, in the middle of his junior year, his grades were *A* in French, *B+* in English, *B*'s in mathematics and science. The accompanying comments from his adviser contained only minor reservations: In physical science, his adviser felt "he is evidently capable of better achievement than his record indicates" and "the total picture seems to call for a more thorough and careful all-around job of work on his part." But the comments of his French teacher overshadowed these reservations:

Michael has a good aptitude for language study and a sensitive feeling for idiomatic French expressions which is marred only infrequently by inaccurate detail. His comprehension would be uniformly excellent if he were not from time to time the victim of his own good inquiring mind, which occasionally and needlessly grows suspicious, ferrets out worrisome subtleties, looks for and finds difficulties where there are none! But Mike is outgrowing these conscientious faults. *He is an engaging young man of unfailing good humor.*

And from his physical education adviser:

Michael has shown interest and eagerness at all times to participate in the activities of the course. His attitude has been excellent, and he has displayed desirable traits of group interaction. His attendance has been excellent.

To his parents, these read like something approaching a model portrait of diligence, conviviality, adjustment, and a praiseworthy striving for larger excellence.

In early spring of his senior year at Fieldston we received what seemed solid confirmation of that impression. One afternoon Luther Tate, then the headmaster at Fieldston, called to tell me that he was dismayed by Michael's inadequate performance in the English College Boards. He feared that it would jeopardize his chances for admission to Harvard but said he was sure he could arrange for a reexamination unless I had any objection. Naturally I expressed my delight and appreciation over his solicitude. Michael fulfilled his expectations by recording a significantly higher score on the second round.

The important fact, of course, was Mr. Tate's assertion of confidence and concern. This seemed new, reassuring evidence that Michael had won both respect and affection at the school's highest levels. It confirmed our belief that our "engaging young man of unfailing good humor" had rather unlimited horizons and a remarkable facility for enlisting both friendship and support in any time of even momentary trouble.

It was not many days later that Michael called me to express his urgent need to see Dr. First about his psychological problems.

IV

Harvard, Drs. Second and Third

MICHAEL entered Harvard in September, 1960, as scheduled. Until then he had never lived away from home. The Fieldston School, as we have noted, was a relatively small, private institution for (with a few exceptions) the children of the prosperous middle class. Mike's best friend from Fieldston and Westport had preceded him to Harvard by one year, and several others from his Fieldston class entered when he did. That should have been a solid nucleus for college life at the beginning, even in what was to seem so large, impersonal, and remote a university as Harvard.

But by the time Michael reached there, withdrawal and loneliness were replacing the lively gregariousness of his high school years. He never talked very much about Harvard during his freshman year, but he gave few signs of finding new friends or enjoying life there. He worked hard, insisting on taking a heavy schedule of difficult courses; he drove his secondhand car back and forth on weekends, sometimes in very bad weather. He seemed to be coping with college, but with effort and without joy.

We knew very little about his life during those months. He never showed us the essays he wrote for freshman English. When we read them some years later, we were struck by the skill, sensitivity, and humor of the writing. (Neither had he ever shown us his many excellent high school papers; he seemed interested in keeping his writing entirely private.)

During the first few months Nancy and I continued to see Dr. Liss occasionally to keep him informed—as well as we could—about Michael's situation and, I suspect, to hear his discreet reassurances. Dr. First remained Michael's long-distance therapist and saw him on his occasional visits to the city. By the

time of Christmas vacation we had become increasingly skeptical about the adequacy of this arrangement, and Michael was
expressing anxieties about the infrequency of consultation.

It was then that Dr. Liss, who had by that time established
some communication with Dr. First, insisted that it was important for Michael to take a Rorschach test. This may have reflected his desire to acquire some additional knowledge of Michael's problems and some basis for an independent appraisal
that might fortify his comments in talking with us.

After the test, as indicated earlier, there was a conspicuous
change in Dr. Liss's mood. He did not attempt to spell out his
reading of the results (and somehow we did not insist that he do
so), but he was quite emphatic in urging that Michael have regular access to a therapist in Cambridge. He volunteered to find
one. Dr. Liss was continuously sensitive to both the ethical issues and the private tensions involved in his role, especially in
view of the irritation both Dr. First and Michael manifested
about his intervention. Yet he was firm on this point and personally selected a therapist.

Perhaps the result was predictable. Dr. Second was a figure
of some distinction, closer in years to Dr. Liss than to Dr. First.
Shortly after he had been brought into the case, I spoke with
him over the telephone and suggested a meeting. He did not
hesitate to propose that we talk when he was to be in New York
shortly thereafter for a psychiatric convention.

He was a genial, hearty, forthright man. In contrast to the
strains immediately evident when I had met Dr. First, I found
conversation with Dr. Second as easy as it had been with Dr.
Liss. Perhaps what made him so appealing at that point was
both an essential tone of optimism and the absence of pretense.
Like Dr. Liss, he did not seem obliged to boast about his record
of achievement or to indicate possession of any unique insights
into the mysteries of the tortured mind.

"He has some of the damnedest," he remarked, referring to
the obsessive images from which Michael was suffering. He said
Michael had a lot of apprehension and shyness about his approaches to girls and added with an amiably mischievous smile;
"I must admit I even tried to give him a few tips."

In general, he exuded confidence. He did not forecast any

prolonged process of treatment; neither did he offer any technical diagnosis. There was a clear quality of reassurance, and I hastened to tell Nancy somewhat exultantly of my relief over his report. While I do not want to indicate that he minimized the difficulties Michael faced, there was an unmistakably different coloration in his estimate; it was partially gray but certainly not grim.

Very soon, however, things began to go badly between Dr. Second and Michael, and that is one of the most distressing phases of this account. For it was almost instantly evident that Dr. First had been less than helpful in the shaping of Michael's attitude and that Michael began with hostilities toward the new man.

The most revealing hint came soon, when Michael was in New York for a weekend and expressed dissatisfaction over the new setup. By that time I knew that any passionate advocacy on my part could only injure Dr. Second's effort. On the other hand, I felt I had to try to persuade Michael to give him a fair chance. Finally Michael exclaimed, "You think that just because a man has written a lot of books it proves he's a good psychiatrist. The two things have no relation."

Although I could hardly undertake to prove the point (nor did I then), Michael obviously seemed to be echoing something he had heard from Dr. First when the transition in treatment took place.

For some reason the authorship of books—or nonauthorship —was a matter of much concern to Dr. First. In one of his sessions with us, suddenly and without any apparent relevance he said, "You know, I'm an angry middle-aged man, too."

I had recently published a book called *Reflections of an Angry Middle-Aged Editor*. A little later he was saying that, if the rules of medical propriety did not prohibit autobiographical works in his field, he could have written many volumes about the successes he had achieved.

It was hard to find any fitting responses to such assertions of pride or insecurity.

The important hint about his concern over literary productiveness was that Dr. Second's role as Michael's doctor proved short-lived. By spring Michael had announced that any further sessions would be useless, and neither Dr. Second nor Dr. Liss felt that we should contest his decision. In a letter from Cambridge Michael wrote:

As you may have gathered, I have never been terribly enthusiastic about Dr. Second. But since he was well thought of by Dr. Liss, I wanted to give it a fair try. However it has reached a point where we quite clearly do not get along well enough together, and I don't feel it makes sense to see him further.

There is nothing to elaborate—I've told Dr. Second exactly what I think, and I don't plan to continue our sessions (he has no particular objections).

Also, I called Dr. First, and he was confident that a new arrangement could be made. I'm quite certain Dr. Second will write you some kind of note (along with his long-overdue bill if you have not received it) I suppose.

Nothing else is new here—you might wish Mother "happy mother's day," since I was not aware of the date when I last wrote.

Love, Mike

Between the lines of that letter we could see more sharply than before the dimensions of the dilemma that Dr. First's role would create in any new therapeutic situation.

So, by the end of the school year, Michael was again being treated by Dr. First. Michael spent that summer of 1961 with us at Westport. Nancy remembers "how tense and drawn he was when I went to Cambridge to help bring his possessions back at the end of the year." He periodically drove the forty miles to Dr. First's Connecticut summer home for what seemed to be a mixture of regular treatment and friendly visit. He was rarely communicative after these trips, but we gathered that after a therapeutic session he would assist in chores on Dr. First's grounds and found this a congenial "home away from home."

Most of the summer he had a job at a local service station and spent his spare time working on his old secondhand car, taking it apart and not being able to put it completely back together again. This was one of the first signs of a change of personality: Mike had always been very skilled at mechanical things; now he was beginning to falter when he became involved in them.

When he began his sophomore year, he was still Dr. First's

patient. He was still uneasy and uncertain, but he seemed to be functioning. He had found it very difficult to share a room during his first year. Now he had a single room in the same house as the friend who was also being treated by Dr. First. He had become extremely sensitive to noise and he used devices to create "white" background sounds. Signs of depression were more evident. He had not involved himself in any extracurricular activities. As the semester got under way, the strains were unabated.

At Thanksgiving vacation his manner was especially unsettling, and Dr. First at last agreed that long-distance therapy was ineffective. Now it was his turn to find a local Cambridge doctor. The man he found was not one he knew but was, he reported, highly recommended to him. By this time it seemed clear that Mike would reject any therapist chosen by a Liss-parent "conspiracy." Dr. Third became the man in charge, with the benefit of Dr. First's blessing.

Dr. Third was only a name to us; he, too, belonged to the school of noncommunication with parents. Indeed, after Dr. First located him and he agreed to become Michael's therapist, I wrote him outlining our view of Michael's history and expressing our readiness to confer with him at any time at his convenience. He did not answer the letter.

However, Dr. Third did discuss it with Michael and soon thereafter this note came from Michael:

Dear Dad:

It looks as if Dr. Third and I might get along all right; at any rate, I think I should continue to see him (I have seen him twice now). He thinks that it is unwise for him to communicate with you, even as regards finances. So he will give me monthly bills which I suppose I will send to you. Anyway, enclosed is the first one.

Love, Mike

Not even Dr. First had insisted upon such a total noncommunication between therapist and parents (in fact, much later Dr. First complained to Nancy that Dr. Third had never communicated with him). The barrier had one crack: We were permitted to mail the checks directly to the doctor.

With the passage of weeks Nancy and I fretted over our isolation. Then, in midwinter of 1962, I found myself scheduled to attend a dinner in Boston. I wrote Michael suggesting that perhaps Dr. Third would now consider it appropriate for us to meet. Michael replied:

> I talked to Dr. Third about your trip to Boston. However, his view is that visits with parents of very young children may be beneficial but that seeing parents of young adults was not helpful. Nevertheless, if you're particularly anxious to visit with him, I don't suppose he would refuse as he simply seems to think that such an encounter would be valueless for me. Anyway, if in spite of this you want to see him, then I suppose you should write him a letter saying so. Apropos of all this, I enclose a bill from Dr. Third. . . .
>
>   Love, Mike

The message seemed brutally plain. Dr. Third would presumably grant us an audience if we persisted in pressing him. But, in his view, this would be a venture in self-indulgence on our part that could not assist (and might possibly obstruct?) his treatment of Michael. It seemed equally clear that Michael accepted this verdict and would resent what the doctor deemed a harmful intrusion.

So we did not pursue the point despite our deep distaste for the procedure. Did it really make sense for a therapist to reject all contact—even an encounter in which he set the ground rules —with parents? Was this crucial to the preservation of a patient's confidence? We were unconvinced and restive, but instead of our airing our doubts, except to each other, I wrote Michael:

> I certainly don't want to press the matter of my seeing Dr. Third. If you feel that things are going well, and Dr. Third feels that a conversation with me would not be helpful to you at this stage, I think it would be best that I drop the idea. I just want both of you to know that I am available if at any time he thinks I can be useful.

As so often in the past, Dr. Liss did his best to help. He established contact with Dr. Third and sought him out to discuss Michael at a winter psychiatric conference. Liss reported to us that he thought well of Third and approved his approach to the case. Grasping that reassurance, we submitted to the arrangement, which was, after all, considerably more sensible than the earlier sporadic long-distance therapy under Dr. First. Michael made it clear that he liked Dr. Third and was seeing him regularly.

As the year went on Michael seemed to become more of a participant at Harvard; Cambridge began to sound like a place he lived in, rather than one to which he was condemned. When he told us, in the spring, that he had obtained a summer job in a laboratory of the Harvard Psychology Department, we became cautiously optimistic. He was now committed to psychology as his major, and the job appeared to confirm the seriousness of his work. Perhaps the unknown Dr. Third did have some answers. But the story was not that simple. To follow it we must go back in time to Dr. First and to the history of Michael's vehicular accidents.

V

A Series of Accidents

On a day near the end of that summer of 1961, when Michael was about to return to Harvard for his sophomore year, there was an unexpected phone call from Dr. First. He came to the point quite quickly: "I wonder if you can afford to buy Michael a Volkswagen." I responded that we could if it seemed important, although my own anxieties about the combustion engine had not dwindled and a small car seemed especially vulnerable. Dr. First said he felt it was very important, indeed, that he believed any effective treatment would be blocked until and unless Michael possessed such a vehicle.

The subject had frequently come up in our home, and we had tried to deflect Michael's insistence. Two summers before he had overturned our car while driving with a young man who was to be his freshman college roommate, Peter Hyman. Both of them were fortunate to walk away from the accident. At the time, it seemed no more than an unlucky skid on an invisible patch of sand on a country road. But in view of the ambiguity about Michael's stability at this juncture, Nancy and I were apprehensive about giving him access to a Volkswagen. Dr. First was emphatic in arguing that his own labors were hopelessly stymied and that acquisition of the car would make Michael a responsive patient.

And so we agreed, despite our skepticism and concern. We assumed—on the basis of that fragmentary knowledge of Freud that all college graduates have acquired—that the issue, as viewed by Dr. First, was related to Michael's need for symbolic assertion of manhood. But what shaped our decision was no thoughtful appraisal of rationalities or risks. It was essentially the awareness that Dr. First was again delivering an ultimatum.

If we turned down his recommendation, he would presumably have proceeded to say that we had fatally obstructed his work. And there was no way to debate the point.

It was at some moment during this period that I expressed to Dr. Liss my fear—and anger—that Dr. First was playing games in which I was inevitably maneuvered into an adversary role with Michael. Thus, when with Nancy's support I balked at Michael's pleas, or demands, for a Volkswagen, Dr. First came to his rescue. Even after our concession, there would remain the unmistakable conclusion that we had failed to comprehend the depth of Michael's need for the car until Dr. First proclaimed its urgency.

Dr. Liss, invariably reserved in voicing what might be construed as criticism of a colleague, replied quietly that psychiatrists could be broadly divided into two groups. There were those, he said, who were convinced that they could work most effectively with patients by using parents as scapegoats; in that process they earned the confidence and intimacy they regarded as essential to effective therapy. There were others—he included himself—who tried to avoid the nourishment of such hostilities and sought to act as a bridge between parents and children, even while acknowledging large areas in which the patient must be assured that there would be no disclosure by the doctor to parents. Characteristically, he refrained from any adverse comment on those who chose the first technique and implored our tolerance for Dr. First's efforts.

So the Volkswagen was bought, and while driving home from Cambridge on a Friday evening several months later, Michael, according to his subsequent account, fell asleep at the wheel and hit an abutment on the Hutchinson Parkway.

When we saw the wreckage of the Volkswagen several days later, it seemed implausible that he had emerged unhurt. In fact, he was able to walk to a telephone and quietly tell us he had been delayed by an accident and was on his way home by train. He required no medical aid. We all had a drink together and then, almost as if nothing had happened, he went to bed. We were left to talk about the folly of our acquiescence in Dr. First's announcement that what Michael most desperately needed to insure the success of his therapy was a Volkswagen.

The next summer, 1962, we were in the midst of another vehicular crisis.

By now Dr. Third, the second Cambridge therapist, was in
charge. Michael was working in the psychology laboratory con-
nected with Harvard and, with the memory of the Volkswagen
accident receding, he had begun a campaign to have us supple-
ment his earnings so that he could buy a motorcycle. Through
the spring semester he had been content to use a bicycle, although unknown to us (and revealed later by Dr. Third) he
had had a series of mishaps with it.

When Michael began pressing for a motorcycle, we asked
him to get Dr. Third's opinion. (Unbelievably, we did not dare
to contest Dr. Third's rules by approaching him directly.) Michael reported that Dr. Third had no opinion to offer. As Michael relayed the message, Dr. Third said it was up to him to
assess whether he felt well enough to drive a motorcycle and up
to us to decide, if Michael really believed he could handle it,
whether to help him buy it.

It is hard to say now whether this abdication was more or
less troublesome than Dr. First's earlier advocacy of the Volkswagen. What seems plain is that, especially in the light of the
previous accident record, there should have been a communal
conversation. But that is not the way Dr. Third (like many of
his colleagues) transacted such business, even though he was
later to tell Nancy that he considered Michael somewhat "accident-prone."

Michael, of course, passionately argued that he was able to
handle a motorcycle safely, but we demurred for many long
weeks.

While Michael was working in the laboratory, we stopped
off to see him on our way back from a brief trip to Martha's
Vineyard. He was very pale and had a bad cough. He took us
around the lab and introduced us to the pigeons in his custody.
The people working with him there seemed very warm and, especially in the case of his middle-aged woman superior, eager to
reassure us about him and the congeniality of his presence.

Later that day we drove out to Concord with him in a quiet
uneasiness and then returned to the rooming house where he
was staying. After dinner, he renewed his fight for a motorcycle.

In some ways this was reminiscent of occasional childhood scenes when he wanted something very badly and could not be diverted. (In the earlier days I comforted myself with the recollection of my own rages when my usually patient father sometimes refused to take me to a baseball game.) But now this was no momentary stubbornness. His face flushed and almost contorted, Michael cried out at one point, "You just don't understand how important this is to me."

Again he seemed to be saying that we were making it impossible for him to live, and he was no longer so young that we could smugly discount such remarks as an adolescent flare-up. He was half crying and half threatening. After he seemed to have exhausted himself in alternate protest and plea, we left him and went to the nearby hotel where we were remaining overnight. He tried to be gracious as he said good night, offering that familiarly heartbreaking intimation of regret that he had uncontrollably stirred up a storm.

Nancy and I were still convinced that it would be imprudent to let him have a motorcycle. It seemed absurd that Dr. Third had refused to consider discussing the decision with us; is that how some psychiatrists protect themselves? But then, what if he had given us a variation of Dr. First's crudely Freudian formula and told us that Michael's therapeutic salvation depended on a motorcycle?

Nancy recalls:

I can see the scene and recall the feeling of screaming inside myself as the repetitive discussion went on and on. The next day we visited him on the job and saw the elaborate electrical devices used to test the rats and pigeons. I could tell by the attitude of the adult workers in the lab that they were concerned about Michael. We left with the issue unresolved and with Mike threatening not to spend any money on food in order to buy the cycle if we failed to give in. With his cough and his tense, drawn appearance, that was a very potent threat and it succeeded.

Some days later, we found ourselves offering a compromise. We agreed to a motorbike, which, because of its smaller dimensions and lower speed, somehow seemed less perilous. Michael accepted the compromise quite joyously, perhaps with some private relief. It was a convenient "good deal" for all of us.

On the morning of October 2, 1962, the telephone rang in Holly's room. (By that time she had acquired the status of a separate line.) Because I rather guessed it was a wrong number, or some dropout suitor of Holly's, I almost neglected to answer it. But this I find hard to do and I picked it up. It was long-distance from Boston, and the caller quickly and quietly identified himself as Dr. Ronald Malt. After establishing that I was Michael's father, he said, "Your son has been in a serious accident."

Michael, riding his motorbike, had collided with a motorbus. As Dr. Malt described it, without any elaboration of the cruel details, I realized he was telling me that there was a chance that Michael might not be alive by the time I reached Boston. At the same time he took pains to say that he believed he could save him. He added that perhaps I should know that he was the doctor who had resewn the arm on a battered youth who had seemingly lost a limb in a widely publicized accident a few weeks earlier. In another circumstance this might have seemed a vanity, but it was stated with hesitant embarrassment, as if he could find no other way of giving me assurance that he was not a doctor who gave up easily.

Nancy and I agreed that she should remain behind to sustain Holly during what we knew would be interminable and possibly intolerable hours.

The flight to Boston was mercifully on schedule. A moment after I walked into the lobby at Massachussetts General, almost dreading to identify myself and make inquiry about Michael, I suddenly saw him being wheeled across the floor. His eyes were open and he seemed to recognize me. I told him he would be all right, that he was getting the best possible medical attention. Again there was that faint, unforgettably gentle smile, as though he were trying to say that I should not be unduly worried. I do not know whether he really heard me.

(In a memoir he wrote three years later, Michael was to say of the accident: "All that's left from that, other than some vague memories, is the scar from a long vertical incision from below my navel to breast level. I've often wished I hadn't lived through it.")

Dr. Malt appeared—a lanky, soft-voiced, comforting man. He could say with greater confidence now that Michael would survive and that he did not even anticipate any permanent wounds. Fortunately the collision had occurred near the hospital; little precious time had been lost before the doctor could begin the rescue operation. He said that when Michael was brought into the hospital he had no blood pressure. When I expressed disbelief that anyone could be saved in that condition, Dr. Malt said, "I wouldn't try it at your age." At last it almost seemed possible to laugh.

On the plane to Boston I had thought often of the shattering call I might have to make to Nancy. Now I could tell her honestly that we had every reason to believe that Michael would live and that he was truly in the hands of a miracle man.

In midafternoon Dr. Malt told me that it was pointless to remain at the hospital. Michael would be under sedation and there would be no chance to see him until the next morning. If any complications developed, the doctor would call me at once. I checked in at a dreary hotel a few blocks from the hospital.

I took a bath, hoping to induce sleep. As I bathed I realized that I had made no effort to reach Dr. Third. I had no clear thought about any purpose he could serve now. Perhaps there was malice in my wanting to be sure he knew the consequence of the motorbike decision, on which he had so cautiously abstained.

I had no difficulty reaching him at his home. When I asked him if he knew what had happened to Michael—the news had been broadcast all afternoon in Boston and even carried on the AP wire—he said he did not. He expressed dismay and then told me that the accident must have occurred while Michael was on his way to keep an appointment with him.

It must now have been about nine o'clock, and all the exhaustion and terror of the day exploded. I asked him whether it had not occurred to him to wonder why a patient had failed to appear and at least to inquire about him late in the day once he had completed his own schedule. Obviously he did not consider that in the line of duty, and I suppose it is quite customary for psychiatric patients to skip appointments without inviting any special curiosity about their absence. But, at that moment, in that setting, his answer seemed to dramatize what often seemed so arrogant and absent-minded about some practitioners in this field of medicine. And so, while he listened tolerantly and without response, I said rather grimly that I hoped he would remember what had happened to Michael when other parents sought without success to communicate with him and were ultimately and indirectly told that such decisions as the purchase of a motorbike were not to be shared with him.

This was the only conversation—I fear it more closely resembled a monologue—I ever had with Dr. Third.

After the accident he did agree to see Nancy, who went to his office for an interview at the time of one of her visits to Michael in the hospital. As Nancy recalls:

It was a strange interview. I told him that we could not understand his past actions. He responded that he had to do what he did in order to keep his patient's confidence. Although the meeting started in an adversary way, it ended on a relatively friendly note. I came away from the interview with the impression of Dr. Third's sincerity and dedication and also with an understanding that 'he would be available for future communication. However, there was no suggestion that there should be family therapy or even occasional meetings with us as parents (as had been the way with Dr. First). Dr. Third was firm in his conviction that it was essential for the treatment that we not be involved and nothing I said in that meeting changed his position.

I did have sporadic communication with him after that, but none that in any way involved us in the therapy, and most of it at times of crisis, when the doctor needed us as much as we needed him. I don't remember any contacts of significance with Dr. Third after the first meeting, although I think we had some relatively casual communication, until the crisis of the spring of 1964. In the interval, Dr. Liss kept in touch with Dr. Third and periodically reported to us. Given the ground rules, we did not discuss Dr. Third with Michael, except in a very casual way, but it did seem clear that Michael had confidence in Dr. Third and was conscientious about seeing him.

Meanwhile, Dr. Malt and his colleagues slowly rebuilt Michael's terribly shattered body, and he gallantly endured a hundred long days before he was permitted to leave the hospital, still on crutches. We visited him twice a week (Nancy and I alternated our trips); nearly always he was striving to conceal the acute pain and wretched discomfort, but occasionally he would exhibit deep depression. As his limbs were gradually restored, it seemed hard to believe that any agonies of the mind could again overshadow the physical ordeal he had gone through.

Nancy recalls that when she saw him in the hospital the day after the accident the first thing he said was, "Mother, it wasn't my fault." However, later he could not remember what happened (the driver of the motorbus admitted having made a bad turn and not having seen the motorbike). It was a relief to Michael to hear this testimony to his innocence.

Inevitably, Michael received a great deal of pain-killing medication at the hospital. The type of medication was varied, we were told, to avoid addiction. We cannot know whether the accident contributed to his later use of drugs and his ultimate trip from marijuana to LSD.

We were in Boston visiting him the weekend of the Cuban missile crisis. He was thinking about what he would do in an air raid, and he had figured out how he would extricate himself from the traction apparatus and get out of the hospital under his own power.

He played the guitar and took up the flute. Although he received many books from friends and relatives, he read very little except the newspapers.

On December 30 his maternal grandparents, Osmond and Helene Fraenkel, saw him, and Osmond wrote in his diary:

Visited Michael at the hospital. He seemed in excellent spirits, hopes to be up on crutches in a week and home the week after that. He talks as though he might go back to college next term. We had a long discussion about cause and effect that, of course, got nowhere. We were pleased to find him interested in such a philosophical subject. We were with him about 1½ hours.

Michael must have literally fought for his life in the immediate aftermath of the crash, and in a sense that is what he was doing for all of the years thereafter in the search that took him to so many therapists and hospitals. But no one he encountered could heal the mental disarray as Dr. Malt and his associates had so skillfully and unbelievably mended his body.

VI

Over the Line

ALMOST FOUR YEARS after Michael began treatment, we were faced with the first overt manifestation of breakdown and his first suicidal "gesture."

Throughout that period, there had been intervals of high hope as well as ominous despondency. He was deeply troubled while working at the psychology laboratory in Boston during the long summer of 1962 that should have been seen as a prelude to crisis. After his crash in October and hundred days at Massachusetts General, he spent about a month at home and then returned to college on crutches in February, 1963. Soon afterward we received characteristically laconic notes assuring us that he did not find it too hard getting around.

While he had been winning no academic laurels or taking any part in extracurricular activities, he finally seemed to be "making it."

(In an essay couched in rather whimsical tones, but perhaps projecting more about his Harvard days than even he guessed at the time, Michael wrote: "Indeed, I am not so uninitiated as to cherish any hopes of knowing who it is who lives just across the hall. God knows, I shall never again make the mistake of answering a stranger in the dining hall; and it is no longer quite so difficult to ride down the elevator without saying a word to either of the three fellow passengers, who are equally silent. . . .")

Innumerable young men have found Harvard an impersonal, somewhat overwhelming institution and managed to get through. At worst, that often seemed to be Michael's situation. Whether the pressures would have been less intense—and the ultimate crack-up less likely—if he had attended a smaller college will never be known. A letter I wrote Michael soon after he reached Cambridge perhaps indicated our continued underestimation of his illness.

I am sorry that we had to have so extended a discussion on finances. [This was a reference to a long conversation about the size of his allowance.] I am sure you understand that Grandpa's illness and the medical expenses involved have made things tighter for us. This does not mean that we are poverty-stricken or that I want you to be worrying about it every moment. It does mean that we have to watch things more closely than I like. . . .

From what I have read in novels, it is customary for a father to offer some great words of wisdom to his son when he goes off to college. I wish I had some, but it seems easier to make public speeches than private ones. Perhaps I am wrong, but I have generally felt that people have to discover both the joys and difficulties of life for themselves, and that no one can blueprint anyone else's existence. All that it seems to me a parent can do, as I think I've tried to say to you before, is to assure you of his affection and loyalty, and to be around if needed.

If Harvard is what it is supposed to be, I envy you; and I hope you have the time of your life. And if it doesn't seem too magnificent at the start, I hope you will be patient with it (and that Harvard will be patient with you!).

Nothing in these homilies, it will be noted, contained any acknowledgment of the emotional problems for which Michael had undertaken treatment the previous spring or of the special burdens he might confront at college as a result of them. The only reference to illness was to that of my father, who, after nearly eighty robust years, had been stricken by a nonmalignant intestinal ailment that was to produce a series of debilitating complications, eventually including the amputation of a leg, until his death five years later. But the reference to money undoubtedly aggravated what was to become Michael's brooding anxiety about the costs of his own illness. Our incredulity about the potential seriousness of Michael's condition was later to be seen by him, we fear, as an evidence of indifference—or insipidity.

In any case, in the aftermath of the miracle wrought by Dr. Malt and his colleagues at the hospital, we had months of quiet rejoicing over Michael's physical recovery and the apparent diminution of emotional stress.

While Michael was in Massachusetts General, Dr. Third said that psychiatric therapy would be unfruitful. It was resumed when Michael went back to Cambridge on crutches for the second semester. He managed to get around uncomplainingly in the New England ice and snow and seemed to become quite cheerful as the semester went on.

Since his convalescence had deprived him of a semester of credit, he decided to attend summer school. He would still be unable to graduate with the class of '64, but he envisaged some graduate work along with the completion of his remaining undergraduate obligations in 1965.

Nancy recalls that when she helped him get settled in a rented room at the beginning of the summer session (he was still using a cane) he was rather jaunty as he said good-by, and he seemed to be looking forward to the throngs of female summer students.

In mid-October of 1963, just a little more than one year after the collision, we went up to Cambridge to attend the Columbia-Harvard football game with Michael. Joining us there were my former secretary, Cecile Eddy O'Brien, and her husband, who had come down from Vermont for the reunion. (Cile had known Michael during the 1950s, when he and Holly often visited the *Post*'s office.) The day has special vividness because we sat a few rows behind President John F. Kennedy, a fortuitous circumstance that seemed to interest Michael as much as the contest. The President was rooting for Harvard with considerable enthusiasm. After the game we went over to Michael's room at Leverett and he produced drinks in a festive atmosphere. Cile observed, as we did, that he appeared remarkably relaxed and a part of things. A few days later I wrote him exuberantly: "I hope you feel as well as you look—it is hard to believe that you are the same guy I was visiting at Mass. General a year ago!"

Our cautious elation lasted for several months, reaching a high point early the following winter (1964), when we learned that Dr. Third had decided that Michael's improvement justified the suspension of regular consultation. Dr. Liss told us that he had encountered Dr. Third at a convention of psychiatrists and that the latter, saying that he had "turned Mike loose," had ob-

served, "I'm holding my breath." We were satisfied to assume
that he had achieved momentous success. Perhaps we also
viewed the news somewhat smugly as a rebuttal to Dr. First's
early pessimism about the duration of Michael's illness.

Nancy recalls that on visits home during this academic year
Michael began to talk about Cambridge in a proprietary way
and sometimes discussed his group of friends at Leverett House
with evident pride as the intellectuals of the house. He also occasionally talked to us about the content of his courses and
liked to engage us in exchanges on philosophical subjects. It
was during this time that another boy we knew who was at Harvard spoke admiringly to us about how many friends Michael
had at school. We knew virtually nothing, however, about what
he was doing from day to day.

Then, suddenly, there was a stunning reversal. But, because
of the absence of any regular access to Dr. Third and the frailty
of our communication with Michael, we were once again appall-
ingly slow to detect—or respond to—what was happening. His
midyear examinations had been completed satisfactorily and, in
the light of the news that Dr. Third no longer deemed regular
visits necessary, we were almost in a mood for celebration.

There arrived a letter from Michael, dated May 18:

Dear Parents:
Unfortunately I flunked my general examination in psychology. I
wasn't exactly surprised; just a little stunned.

Right now I'm trying to study physics "in spite of it all," as that's
the next exam on the agenda. Since I've done at least a modicum of
work in physics (it's that kind of subject—you can't avoid it completely!) I'd be a little annoyed with myself if I don't at least pass.

On the lighter side: now that there is a more or less real cause for
rioting, no rioting has as yet broken out.° Specifically, it turns out
that Harvard is the largest stockholder in a Mississippi Utilities Company, and that the officials of the company are (some of them) on the
White Citizens Council. But it only seems to be bothering the *Crim-
son* at this point!

In short (not being the riot-starting type), I can only *hope* for a
riot to distract me from work.

                                                    Love, Mike

   ° Cambridge had been the scene of several old-fashioned "spring" student riots, without the political overtones of events later in the decade.

Disappointed as we were by his failure in the examination, the letter did not invite alarm. Dr. Liss had warned us often in our informal talks that there would be detours on the road to recovery, and Michael's tone seemed reassuringly casual. Since his general state seemed far more important than the result of any examination, I wrote him in the same vein of unconcern:

Naturally we were sorry to hear about the general psych. exam; to paraphrase your words, we are surprised but not stunned. We trust the rest will go better. Meanwhile, at such a moment please bear in mind that an F will not loom very large in your life when you're telling your grandchildren your life story. I have no doubt bored you on numerous occasions with reminiscences of the year at Columbia when I got two F's in one semester; I am not urging imitation but merely suggesting that you take the long view. End of sermon.

We had no way of knowing, since Dr. Third still avoided volunteering information to us, that the deterioration was far graver than Michael's note disclosed. Not until Michael came home in early June, in time to attend Holly's graduation from the Dalton School, did he spell out the full details of his academic debacle: He had not only flunked his general but obtained medical permission to escape two other exams; he had little academic credit to show for the whole semester.

His demeanor seemed relatively calm, open, and friendly. However, he did say, again without any grim flourishes, that he had gone back into therapy and that Dr. Third wanted him to return to Cambridge for some intensive, extended sessions during the next few weeks. Michael said he had arranged for an off-campus room. So, after remaining with us for about a week, he headed back for Cambridge.

About two weeks later Michael telephoned Nancy at her office. He said he was returning to New York at once and that Dr. Third wanted her to accompany him back for a joint session on the following Tuesday. He offered no explanation but said that Dr. Third was very insistent about seeing her.

He arrived in the evening, looking haggard and solemn. It was Friday and we left for a weekend in Westport together. Along the way Michael sat stolidly and silently in the car. He remained in bed throughout the next day. Finally, before din-

ner, Nancy went up to his room. There he told her what had
produced the summons from Dr. Third.

On Thursday of that week, after a session with the doctor, Michael had gone back to his room and swallowed a large, presumably dangerous number of pills. Then he had taken himself
to the university infirmary, where his stomach was pumped. He
remained overnight. The next morning Dr. Third visited him
there, ordered him home, and told him to come back with his
mother the following week.

There was a plausible, if painful, reason for Dr. Third's proposal that Nancy, rather than both of us, participate in the conference. Clearly my telephone conversation with him on the
night of Michael's Cambridge collision had been as disastrous as
my early telephone encounter with Dr. First.

It was a long weekend in Westport as Nancy and Michael
prepared for the journey to Boston. For the first time—at least
since his rare, seemingly conventional childhood outbursts of
temper—Michael explosively lost control in our presence. He
had heard me talking to a friend of ours and inviting the friend
and his wife to spend a few days at our Westport home. I was
explaining that Nancy might have to be away for a few days
during our approaching vacation. As soon as I hung up Michael
stormed into the room exclaiming, "Oh, you're afraid to be alone
in the house with me. . . ." I tried to dispel that idea, but he
walked out, slamming the door so hard that it splintered. Then,
a few moments later, he asked us to go to the beach to give him
a chance to regain control of himself.

He joined us on the beach in about half an hour. His face
was white and mournful. He expressed regret for his outburst
but said, "You'll have to expect that to happen for a while."

There were no further incidents over the weekend; neither
was there any real conversation. Then Michael and Nancy left
for Boston. She writes of that trip and its sequel:

I talked to Dr. Third at length while Mike went for a walk. Dr.
Third said that this had been a suicidal gesture; but that he did not
take it too seriously; lots of adolescents did such things. He said that
Mike had talked to him about perhaps needing to be hospitalized, but
that he (Dr. Third) thought this was not necessary. Up to then it had
never occurred to me to even consider such a possibility; I had taken

it for granted that Mike would get better as time went on, and that the only real question was how long he would need to continue in therapy. Dr. Third talked of Michael's adolescent problems (although Michael was then twenty-two, he said it was a kind of delayed adolescence); he said Michael was having an identity crisis and indicated that it might be wise for him to take a year off from school. He mentioned that Mike had experimented with drugs, but said there was no addiction involved. It turned out that Dr. Third was due to go on vacation starting within about two weeks and would be unable to see Michael for a month. He said that Michael should go home again, and we did.

For the next week or ten days there was a steady worsening. There were a number of episodes in which Michael flew off the handle and expressed hostility and anger in a way we had never seen. He was not in any way deluded or psychotic as we later came to understand the term. He was angry, particularly at his father (on one occasion threw a glass at him), tense all the time, unable to organize himself. I was on the phone with Dr. Third, I can't remember how many times, and Michael talked to him a number of times. We had a lot of talk at home but most of it was a running battle. Jimmy was taking a week off and he and Mike spent much of that time uneasily in the country. One day Mike decided to go up to Boston to see Dr. Third but turned around and returned home at the last minute because he didn't feel up to it. Finally, he did fly to Boston to see Dr. Third.

That afternoon the doctor called me (it was around June 28 or 29, and he was to leave for vacation on July 1). He said that he had found Mike in such bad shape that he had sent him to the hospital, so that, as he put it, Michael could be in good hands for a month while the doctor was on vacation. Afterward, he and Michael would resume the therapy. Mike had taken a taxi to the hospital and, by telephone arrangements with Dr. Third, he was admitted.

That was the first of the six periods of hospitalization during the next five years.

Not until much later, when we found the memoir he was to write in his East Village refuge, did we begin to get any real glimpse of what that sad spring had been like. Certainly Dr. Third either knew little of the story or did not share his knowledge with Nancy, even when he finally turned to her for what often seemed like advice.

These are fragments from Michael's own account of that chaotic spring preceding his first hospitalization:

At any rate, that last semester was my worst. The previous one
had been all right, but I couldn't get involved in my work second
semester—but then I'd never really be studious. Also, I was smoking a
lot of pot, even day in and day out for some weeks; that's no way to
accomplish anything. And, I had generals to pass for which I was ill
prepared from previous years; still, I hardly studied for them at all; I
tore up an important set of notes about a week before the exam. I
really had it in for myself that semester. Besides, I was more interested in having philosophical bull sessions with Quentin, or psychological ones (of the tender-minded variety) with Steve, who was a
pretty mixed-up pre-med student. I also played the flute a lot in Leverett's basement and wasted time in sundry other ways. I ended up
by flunking one course and getting excused from two other final examinations.

. . . All this happened while I was "regressing in the service of
the ego," though it wasn't actually doing my ego a bit of good. For
instance, one day I'd have to go see Dr. Third; but I'd be afraid of
crossing some not too dangerous streets; walking down the stairs to the
subway was frightening—I clung to the banister; I was afraid of falling onto the tracks. All the while I was feeling pleasantly sad during
most of the day; at night I'd have more irrational fears, like that of
cutting myself.

And I could hardly work at all, though I don't think that really
bothered me. It wasn't that I couldn't make preparations—I did more
research for a psychology paper than I ever had, but I couldn't produce anything. Each morning I would try to write something, but I
was plagued by the thought that nothing I wrote was my own; and I
was never satisfied with the amount of research I'd done. After one
month of this, one Saturday I had only a drink or two, but got quite
high, I started to write. I wrote an absurdly short paper—two pages
long; it had nothing to do with the course, or with any of my preparation. I flunked the course.

On psychiatric grounds, I was excused from two other final examinations, which means you have to take them the next year—but I
never did. The only course I passed was physics, with a C.

Further, my analyst was going on vacation in a few weeks. I
started getting slightly suicidal; I'd been taking tranquilizers, and one
day I finished the bottle—thirty-four times the regular dose (I later
found out that they probably wouldn't have killed me). But I quickly
put on my shoes, for I suppose I'd been napping, and I went to the

Harvard clinic. They kindly pumped out my stomach, which I rather enjoyed because there was a very warm nurse holding my hand and saying everything was really better than I thought it was, which was a lot of crap. So they put me in a room of my own—they have a room reserved for nuts; I stayed there twenty-four hours.

As far as we know, this was the first warning that Michael's life might end in suicide—unless what Dr. Third depicted as "accident-prone" tendencies are to be retroactively read as something more sinister. Certainly nothing in Dr. First's early diagnosis had contained any hint of this direction. And even as he arranged for Michael's hospitalization during his own vacation, Dr. Third was minimizing the incident in his meeting with Nancy. He seemed to regard the projected internment as a minimal security measure during his absence.

Yet this must now be seen as a critical turning point. Michael was no longer one of many troubled young men receiving psychiatric help. He was a "mental patient" confined to what in an earlier time would have been called an asylum. His own view of himself was inescapably transformed by the transition, and suicide—as his actions there and subsequent unpublished writings were to show—loomed steadily larger in his mind.

Among the infinity of questions to which we will never know the answers is whether the timing of Dr. Third's vacation, with the abrupt alteration in the therapeutic cast of characters, was one of many misfortunes that shadowed and shaped the rest of Michael's life.

VII

The First Mental Hospital

To A VISITOR, Pleasant View seemed a quiet, serene place. Its green grounds were spacious and well manicured, reminiscent of an Ivy College campus, and its atmosphere—to the outsider— conveyed little of the grim institutional grayness that we were to encounter elsewhere. Nancy and I each visited Michael there only once, on separate occasions; thereafter we were told that it would be preferable if we remained away for a while.

Nancy recalls her arrival in early July:

The door to the ward had to be unlocked before Michael could come out to join me. This was my first contact with a hospital social worker—she had called to make arrangements about things like getting clothes to the hospital—friendly, whatever she could do to explain, and so forth.

After Mike was released from behind the locked door, we walked around and went to the snack bar and talked, not about anything important. He looked quite well, seemed reasonably calm, but we really didn't communicate. Then I was interviewed for about an hour by the doctor who was his "therapist," a rather Germanic young man, who asked me many questions about early childhood (at what age he toilet trained is one of the questions I remember) and told me absolutely nothing. Then I had an interview with the doctor in charge and the social worker. Though technical terms were used, no diagnosis was mentioned, but it was clear that these people did not consider Michael's stay at the hospital simply a holding operation pending the return of Dr. Third from vacation. They said that he was "flooded with fears," "quite sick," but not "psychotic," and that he definitely belonged in a hospital. The message seemed to be that he acutely needed help, and that they could provide it.

I began to realize that there was a great difference between the approach of private therapists and hospital therapists. That realization was reinforced later, when Dr. Third returned, and it became apparent that he did not think Michael needed to stay in the hospital while the hospital people insisted he did.

My visit followed Nancy's. The two doctors with whom I spoke were earnest, intense, and guarded. They asked more questions than they answered and, as in talking with Nancy, they withheld any decisive judgments or forecasts. Then Michael and I went out for an early dinner at the snack bar. Our conversation was subdued but friendly. Michael, while appearing less distraught and disorganized, expressed skepticism about the value of hospitalization. Afterward, on July 22, I wrote him: "I hope things will go better; I wish you felt as good as you look, but perhaps you underestimate the benefits of the place."

Now it seems that I was forever writing him such pep-notes, and perhaps they confirmed his recurrent outcry, in moods of desolation during ensuing years, that we were hopelessly incapable of discerning or discussing the anguish of his illness.

Certainly neither of us returned from Pleasant View with any sense of desperate overtones; in effect we were marking time, waiting for the return of Dr. Third. Nevertheless, what the hospital doctors said could not be forgotten. At one point we were told by the social worker, with whom Nancy intermittently conversed by telephone, that Michael had been "acting out" and had been transferred to a heavily restricted ward. She indicated there had been another tentative self-destructive "gesture," but there was again no intimation of gravity.

A little less than a year later, however, in his never-completed memoir, these were some of the somber recollections of that long summer that he set down:

Those two months I spent at Pleasant View were the most miserable of my life; I was uncomfortable day in and day out. I can't stand being among a group for very long, and each meal meant sitting at a table with other patients; during the rest of the day there was literally no place to be alone, except when, later on, I didn't have a roommate —but they often forced me out of my room. Also, I didn't like many of the patients or staff, though I preferred the latter. Furthermore, if you wanted to watch TV, you had to sit in the TV room, where there were always lots of other people; but I could never watch television —I couldn't keep my eyes on the screen, of if I did, I never could pay enough attention; I had irrational fears that, if I let my eyes rest on

another patient, the staff would think I was a homosexual, which was
crazy—they wouldn't have cared much even if I were one, anyway.
So I was continually tense when in that room, which was a lot of the
time, and nobody realized how miserable I was.

When I first saw, after having met him that once, Dr. Steinman,°
I wasn't saying much, mainly crying, sometimes about Third's departure; I was really pretty out of it. Also, whenever I talked to Dr.
O'Reilly, I insisted on anticipating all his thoughts, though I had
crazy notions about what was going on in his head—I don't remember
what I thought, but I have a dim recollection that I was always very
far afield.

I began to like Dr. Steinman, whom I saw five times a week for
the first month, and three times for the three or four weeks after-
wards; I eventually stopped seeing him altogether, by mutual consent; that was after Dr. Third got back. I was more open with Dr.
Steinman than I'd ever been with Dr. Third, which was depressing,
especially when Dr. Third's return approached. In fact, this was the
most difficult period at the hospital, since I started having very detailed recollections of my previous sessions with Third. I seemed to
discover, a little more each day, that we had never understood each
other—that Third had had false ideas about what I was like, how capable I was, and so on; I also thought I had, unintentionally, misrep-
resented myself. Besides, I began to think Third was wrong about
most everything, which was a switch; I thought that he was a mega-
lomaniac, who could never be made to see the truth, and the truth
was unpleasant, besides, mainly having to do with my never being
honest with myself, or planning anything important or necessary, or
not working hard enough at school; though, looking back, I exaggerated all this immensely. Still, I managed to convince myself that I
shouldn't see Dr. Third anymore; but I could never admit that to the
hospital doctors, as I was afraid I'd change my mind and they
wouldn't let Third see me. Anyway, about the time Dr. Third was to
come back from Europe, I started strangling myself—with ties, shirts,
razor cord—whatever I could get my hands on, which wasn't much. I
told the doctors what I was doing, and occasionally they'd put me on
suicide precaution: door open, one-to-one off the hall, and frequent
checks (attendants visiting you each fifteen minutes).

Finally Dr. Third came to see me, and I had so much I wanted to
say to him, most of it not very pleasant, that I could only talk
obsessionally—what was going to happen to my teeth—how many

° The names of doctors mentioned in this segment are fictitious; Michael invented them.

cavities did I have (I was too nervous to brush my teeth properly, because of other patients being in the bathroom, or because I was afraid
they might enter) and other such trivia; I think Dr. Third thought I
was totally distracted, though that wasn't at all true; during the day
I'd think quite rationally about meaningful things—I merely couldn't
communicate very well to the doctors, though I talked quite normally
to some of the younger patients, when I did talk at all.

Anyway, after my first visit with Dr. Third I tied a guitar strap
pretty tight around my neck (Ronald had been good enough to bring
his guitar—I asked my parents not to bring mine, for one silly reason
or another); I had even told the head nurse that I had this guitar
strap, and maybe he ought to confiscate it, but they didn't take me
very seriously there, some of them. In the meantime, I'd put my hand
through a window in my room (I had a single then); and the last
strangling left some large red blotches on my neck, so they gave me
specials (your own nurse) that weekend, to try to get me to talk, but I
wouldn't partly because I always underrated the significance of my
suicidal gestures, and I didn't want them to know I wasn't pretty intent on taking my life. Then they transferred me to the maximum-se-
curity ward, Manor House. That meant a new group of patients, security screens on the windows, and more precautions—people watching
you all day and night, and electric lights over your bed when you
went to sleep at night. All that just because they wanted to keep me
alive, though I'd actually asked one of the student nurses—one I liked
—to untie the knot, which she wasn't able to do, and several aides
came in and cut the strap.

This was a rambling, disjointed retrospect, but it was clearly
not fantasy, whatever the embroidery of detail. Too many of the
episodes have been independently confirmed. What seems important now is the evidence that the suicide "gestures" were
multiplying, even as our own confusion—and that of the doctors
—increased.

Thus, after Dr. Third's return from Europe, Nancy spoke
with him by telephone several times. She found that he and the
hospital therapists were in disagreement but that he was no
longer optimistic about Michael's early release. "Of course there
is always a regression associated with hospitalization," he said,
leaving us to wonder to each other how the cycle was to be broken, especially when there was disagreement between the private therapist and the hospital staff.

Michael broke the deadlock by taking matters into his own hands.

By his own account, he had decided that continued incarceration was unbearable:

All I did by this time was to pace up and down the hall all day long and at night, too. Nobody knew what to make of that; but it just meant, if anything, that I wanted out. I knew I didn't have a chance of getting discharged through a court hearing; I couldn't talk sensibly enough, and you didn't stand a very good chance even if you did appear all right in front of the judge.

I was, and had been, however, taking great pains not to appear suicidal, and I was absorbed completely in this effort. I tried not to do anything suspicious with the cord of my electric razor—though someone always had to watch me shave (in fact, I had to be watched whenever I went to the bathroom!). . . .

The most terrible part of all this was that I "know" I was sane but merely upset in front of the authorities; and I wasn't getting any less upset either. I've wondered a little just how well I actually was, but I have no regrets about leaving. . . .

One weekend my parents were supposed to visit, something I didn't look forward to, but which I pretended to be happily anticipating to Dr. O'Reilly. By this time I really felt a failure, and seeing my parents wasn't going to help. I think maybe Dr. O'Reilly had a glimpse of that fact. But Thursday of that week [before Labor Day] I decided to ask the doctor if I couldn't go to Cronin's for a bite to eat; I hardly expected him to agree, but thought that maybe the act I'd put on about wanting to see my parents would lead Dr. O'Reilly to believe I wouldn't try to escape. This was one of the few conscious acts I'd put on; there were lots of other acts that were entirely out of my control and very disturbing; e.g., a week or two after I first came to Pleasant View, I asked Dr. Penney what he thought my problem was, and he said, "You are troubled by indecisiveness and anxiety," the first part of which was certainly true—I had trouble deciding which shirt to wear—immediately after which I, unintentionally, acted much more anxious than I had since I was first admitted, and right in front of Dr. Penney, as if to show him how right he was; it was several hours later that I'd realized what I'd done. Also, I had lots of meaningless routines which I think suggested to some members of the staff that I had some plot to kill myself—that's what they were looking for, anyhow. One night when I really did have such a plot—I was rooming with Mr. Eddingtom at the time . . . I put the cord of my electric razor in my pocket, planning to strangle myself in the bathroom when I got the chance; I was intensely worried lest someone should find the cord and think I was planning to strangle Mr. Edding-tom; in fact, Mr. Eddingtom himself may have seen the cord, but I doubt that now (probably some kind of hidden fantasy that I'd be protected from myself, and also punished, perhaps).

At any rate, after I'd lied and said I wasn't having any suicidal thoughts, Dr. O'Reilly actually agreed to let me out, with the warning that "If you become paralyzed, be sure to come right back." But it was a relief, getting out of there.

I hadn't any particular escape plans; I didn't know where to go. Previously my old friend, Ronald, had frowned on the idea of my es-caping ("Isn't there some more conventional manner of departing?"), so I didn't know whether to call him, but I did (what harm was there in it, other than wasting a little time—I had about six hours until I was expected back); but Ronald wasn't home. In the meantime I'd taken what I had out of the bank, one hundred dollars, so I could travel as far as necessary. There was a fairly well founded rumor that if you escaped for ten days, you were free; that sounded pretty easy. I went to the train station, where I paced a little more, but decided not to return to New York right away; I also tried to find a friend at Brandeis but couldn't. I ended up going to a friend who'd rented me a room the summer before; I did my best to tell him the whole story. William thought I ought to go back to the hospital, as he wasn't so sure I was as well as I thought myself to be; but he agreed to keep me, and his wife was nearly delighted at the idea. In fact, during the last few minutes I had to decide what I was going to do, Christine cooked a good meal for William and me, and that was that; that was also the way I was making decisions then, unfortunately.

I had a room of my own, from which I occasionally emerged to visit William or Christine; but I didn't dare go outside, since people from Pleasant View often visited Cambridge, and for all I knew the police were alerted. So, William and Christine did all my shopping, she being almost nine months pregnant, no less, and no less amazing for her vigor. I spent most of my time pacing and eating, dropping a lot of food on the floor, and picking it up again and eating; I didn't care much about germs anymore, though I used to. All the time I was very worried about school, which was to start in a few weeks; I didn't know whether or what to write my tutor. I thought quite a bit about strangling myself; I was continually tense, and hopeless.

But William's mother-in-law was supposed to come in a few days, and though that wasn't a problem for them, I thought I ought to leave; I think their kids were returning, too, so it would have been awfully noisy (six and seven years old). Besides, I had a small room; I needed more pacing room!

Anyway, one night the two of them drove me to the airport; they'd really been terrific, his wife pregnant and all, and he working on an overdue Ph.D. thesis, Christine doing the typing; but I suppose it was an oddity, having an escaped mental patient at your house; or maybe just French hospitality, as Christine was French. Mainly, they were a good couple. They paid for half of my food and didn't charge me any rent.

I was afraid the police would pick me up at the airport (though that didn't seem too likely) especially since I'd been A.W.A. (absent without authority) for several days. But I later found out that only a mild alert had been sent out, as I'd called my parents to tell them I was in good hands, and not to come visit me that weekend; my father didn't want the whole affair made public and convinced the doctors not to put out an All Points Bulletin, which perhaps they otherwise would have done; and that would have meant staying the full ten days at the Renaults'.

I felt very strange on the plane, as if I were not really alive; I was to know more of that feeling later. But it was good to be leaving.

After walking a few blocks back from the subway from the airport, I got home; no one was in, but the superintendent got me a key; I think this was a Saturday or Sunday. I waited for my family to come back from the country.

Thus Michael had engineered his escape from Pleasant View.

He had, in fact, called Nancy at her office on that Friday to tell her that our planned journey would be pointless; he said he had left the hospital and was with friends, whom he would not identify. He urged her not to worry about him.

I called the hospital as soon as Nancy reached me and was startled to discover that the institution was unaware that he was missing. After checking, an official there ascertained that Michael had been given an all-day pass to go to Boston in recognition of his favorable progress (the phrase was "because he was doing so well"). His self-described "act" had indeed confounded the doctors.

It was the immediate impulse of the hospital authorities to ask the police to put on an alert. I asked for time to try to locate Dr. Third. Since we had heard from Michael, we were reluctant to make him a hunted man, subject to the harassment that might occur in the process of apprehension. Rightly or wrongly, we considered his phone call to Nancy a considerate action that would be poorly repaid by sending the police after him. Perhaps we were also uncertain whether there was any further purpose in hospitalization. After all, the most recent reports, produced by Michael's carefully rehearsed performance, had been optimistic and the doctors themselves seemed to have disparate views of the case.

Nancy undertook to reach Dr. Third. Unlike a number of psychiatrists whom we have vainly tried to find at critical moments during non-office hours, Dr. Third had someone on duty who was authorized to reach him in emergency situations; soon he was calling us back. He agreed that the police should not be summoned and persuaded the hospital to withhold at least temporarily any request for a major alert.

In Westport we waited vainly throughout Saturday for another call from Michael, one of us at the phone at all times. By midday Monday the silence was increasingly nerve-racking. Then, on a wild chance, we decided to telephone our apartment in New York. Michael answered it. He had been there for more than twenty-four hours.

We rushed back to the city. He seemed more weary than agitated, but he was firm about not going back to Pleasant View. This was the first of many comparable scenes involving escapes from hospitals, but on this occasion we were not disposed to disagree. Neither was Dr. Third, although the hospital officialdom strongly recommended return. Can one hope to know who was right? It is reasonable to suppose that the decision warranted a full-scale conference at which Nancy and I could listen to the divergent opinions of Dr. Third and the hospital therapists. It did not occur to us to request it. By then, we were sure that such a summit meeting would have been deemed unthinkable on either side, and we were wandering aimlessly in the middle, reduced at times to quarrels with each other that reflected our mutual frustration about the maddeningly elusive protocol of the psychiatric establishment.

VIII

Deeper into Darkness

Now, HAVING SUCCESSFULLY FLED Pleasant View, Michael was back at home with us. But escape from hospital confinement did not bring him release from his oppressive private prison, and another harrowing interval began.

As the initial satisfaction of the escape from Pleasant View wore off, he was once again jittery, disoriented, full of hypochondriacal unease about small physical matters. He frequently compared himself disparagingly to other patients he had met. He recalled what seemed to be their facility for small talk and social informality, and even such diversions as card-playing. He seemed to have forgotten entirely the gregarious years of his early adolescence, when he exuberantly gave and attended parties. Now he spoke as if there had never been such a time and of his faded hope that there ever could be.

Through much of September, he was grappling with the issue of whether to return to Harvard for the fall semester. He made frequent phone calls to Dr. Third; then he and Nancy drove to Cambridge for a consultation. But Dr. Third would not venture a recommendation. By that time, our earlier impression that the therapist was more often turning to Nancy for counsel than volunteering his own was being repeatedly confirmed.

After the inconclusive meeting, Michael kept a suitcase packed in his room, as if resolved each day that he would set out for Harvard the next morning. Finally it became clear that he could not face the prospect of returning to school. Dr. Third, who had professed to see sufficient improvement the previous winter to discontinue regular therapy, now concluded that Michael should remain home, find a therapist in the city, preferably a woman, and get a job.

After that decision was reached, Nancy drove Michael to

Cambridge to clear out his room.

"It was a sad trip," Nancy remembers. "On the way, trying to explain what he was going through, Michael burst into tears, and I had to pull off the highway so that both of us could try to compose ourselves. Ironically, when we got there, we found that the boy who was to take over Mike's room had been seeing the university doctors to get clearance to return after having broken down the previous semester and gone into a hospital. He told Mike that after leaving the hospital he had pulled himself together by spending the summer playing tennis and reading.

"When Mike told me that, I could see that he was thinking: 'I wish it would be that easy for me.' "

Once again Michael's unfinished autobiography unfolds in depth the depression that we encountered each day that autumn. After describing his escape from Pleasant View and his return to his old room in our apartment, he wrote:

The next month or two is hard for me to remember, but it was a time almost as bad as at Pleasant View. I paced all the time, overate tremendously, and slept, forcing my eyelids shut until the muscles hurt. At this point, anything my parents said made me irrationally angry, though sometimes I could understand why, like when my father said, "I took a calculated risk in hushing up your escape." I seriously wondered how he made his "calculations."

Also I was agitated all day long; even taking walks didn't help. At least, I'd been discharged from Pleasant View in the meantime— before my ten days were up, I think; also, it turned out that we had more insurance than I'd thought.

Every day, or nearly so, I'd wake up afraid, sometimes of nothing in particular, sometimes because my mother was leaving for work, which is pretty sick, I suppose. But I felt an urgency, of the all-day variety, about two decisions, and I contemplated taking various poisons, shooting myself, jumping from the window much of the time. But somehow I wasn't as daring as I'd been at the hospital, I think because there wasn't somebody to take care of me the way they would have at Pleasant View. I never got those blotches around my neck, anyway.

Every night I would lie down on my bed—I never undressed then, or got under the covers, I used the bedspread to cover myself— and my father would come into my room. The lights were always turned off, and I never said anything, so I guess he thought I was sleeping, which I would be an hour or two later on. I wanted to talk to him, but I just couldn't. I remember one night they were playing Shakespeare on the radio, and I was sad because I couldn't understand a lot of the vocabulary. I'd tried talking with my father that evening, but we were in two far-apart worlds. I know I made it pretty tough on my parents then, but not as tough as I made it for myself. Life wasn't worth living, not one minute of it.

I began to think that, if I was going to stay in New York—and it looked like inertia was winning out—I ought to take a place of my own, which my parents were willing to allow and pay for. When I first returned, I told them that being home, around all my relatives, was the crux of my every problem, and that no one was to know my address when I moved out, which I planned on doing a lot sooner than I finally did.

Unhappily, that is where Michael's own chronicle ends. For the remainder of his life, he wrote only the poetry of melancholy, unrequited love, or unbridgeable detachment, and random notes of despair.

But the battle was not over.

After our agreement that he would not go back to Harvard that fall and his lapse into the oblivion he described, he did begin to scan advertisements for both prospective apartments and jobs. Yet each time he responded to an ad his effort was perfunctory, and he would return home even more desolate and aloof. On many days he did nothing except eat, sleep, and intermittently play his flute. He shunned any encounters with friends who telephoned; he rarely left the apartment for any social engagements; when we had infrequent visitors—most of whom he had known and even including close relatives—he made only brief appearances or did not emerge from his room at all.

I think back to that sentence in his memoir: "I'd tried talking with my father that evening, but we were in two far-apart worlds." I have thought often of the faltering starts of the conversations that never really began or that ended so abruptly because of his conviction that I could not fathom the nature of his despair or provide any adequate response.

Yet even as Michael felt that I could not glimpse the mysteries of his universe, both Nancy and I were inhibited by dread of using the wrong word or phrase and, perhaps even worse, of not knowing where to begin. This was a real curse of the insulation decreed by the therapeutic procedure—that somehow Michael had derived from it the conviction that we inhabited separate, impenetrable worlds, and that neither Nancy nor I could hope to understand his tortured realm. I recall the innumerable nights when I went into his room, as he noted, before going to sleep and, finding the lights out and hearing no sound, quietly retreated lest I awaken him, yet each time imagining or hoping that on the next night he would be up and wanting to talk.

With the final decision not to return to Harvard, there was now the problem of seeking another therapist for Michael in New York. Once again it was Dr. Liss, faithful friend as well as counselor, who undertook the search. In line with Dr. Third's suggestion, for reasons never elaborated, that a woman therapist was now indicated, Dr. Liss finally found Dr. Fourth.

She willingly met with us and told us something of what she thought was happening. It was her view that Michael was in an extreme state of "depersonalization" (was this a euphemism for *schizophrenia?*). He also had distressing physical discomfort, such as a feeling that "his skin was too tight." On one occasion, she said, he wept almost continuously through their session, a degree of anguish that he resolutely hid from us. She expressed confidence that she could help him but emphasized her belief that it was important for him to get a job and find an apartment of his own.

But Michael still seemed paralyzed about going through the motions required to obtain work. Finally, he reluctantly agreed to let us "use our influence" in his behalf. I talked with a long-time friend of ours, Richard Sachs, head of Sachs Quality Stores. He had known Michael and was fond of him and quickly agreed to see him.

They met late in September and this is Dick's recollection of their talk:

We talked for close to an hour about many things—why he was taking a leave of absence from Harvard, what ideas he had about his future life and career, what kind of work he might find interesting and/or stimulating, and what kind of things interested and entertained him.

Mike was frank but clearly unsure of himself. He couldn't "do" anything, wasn't "trained," didn't want "charity." If he could get a job that didn't require experience or special training, he'd give it a try.

We talked about flute playing. Mike said he played—and was pretty good—and we had a brief discussion about the semantic merits of *flutist* as opposed to *flautist*.

Mike was very firm in his opposition to accepting a job for which he wasn't qualified. I had suggested some training in our buying office as a junior assistant, a position for which we are always looking for bright, green young men who want a potentially rewarding career in retailing. I pointed out that he was bright and could, in a short time, learn enough in our buying office to make a good contribution.

No avail.

This brought to mind a conversation I had with Michael in Westport one summer a few years earlier when he was working in a service station. He wanted to get the job himself and not try to do anything for which he wasn't trained.

I finally suggested the possibility of starting as a credit clerk. He accepted the idea that this wasn't charity and agreed to start work at $57.50 per week.

After a few difficult days during which Michael expressed uncertainty about his capacity to cope with even the limited demands of that job, he seemed to achieve a tolerable stability in the routine. He saw Dr. Fourth regularly, and he emerged from his self-imposed exile and began seeing old friends, one of whom helped him locate an apartment on East Ninety-sixth Street and Lexington Avenue. He came home for dinner about once a week.

Some time in December, we gave a small cocktail party and Nancy recalls that Michael arrived "looking wonderful in a very respectable new suit he had bought." He had a long, warm conversation with Dave Dubinsky, the labor leader and cherished friend, about their mutual attachment to bicycles. Michael no longer seemed intimidated about meeting strangers. He was lively and communicative, if anything, "almost too exuberant," as Nancy recalls. But the contrast with his September gloom and remoteness was so heartening that we did not pause to wonder whether there might be anything except favorable portent in his new animation. Our optimism was heightened by glowing comments I received from Dick Sachs about Michael's progress at work.

Dick has written us of that period, confirming our recollection of his cheerful early appraisal:

It soon became clear that Michael was too good to stay very long in a job as simple and undemanding as elementary credit checking. He agreed after about two months that he could complete his assignments pretty much by rote. He was ready to move into the buying office as a junior clerk but wouldn't accept a wage increase until he felt it was really merited. The transfer is normally a promotion and merits a raise.

And so, as in the autumn of 1963, we thought we could glimpse the beginnings of a full recovery. Michael must have had some comparable visions; it was during that time that he began his chronicle of his hospitalization, as if confident that he was describing a completed chapter of suffering.

He apparently recorded his own estimate of progress in letters to Dr. Third. A note after he had begun treatment with Dr. Fourth elicited this reply: "I'm glad some of the acute misery is over for you. Good luck with the rest of it. I think time is on your side."

Then there was a later letter from Dr. Third that said:

Don't be annoyed. My not writing is not from lack of interest. I've been very busy. Apparently you have too! Besides, your notes don't really need any comment from me. It sounds as if you are continuing to grow. The only concern is that you might do too much too fast, in which case your judgment may seem somewhat shaky.

And then, again from Dr. Third, perhaps this prophetic one: "Sorry to be so slow in returning this. [Content unidentified.] Hope things continue to go well. Watch yourself. There'll be downs as well as ups."

What seemed a further expression of self-confidence was Michael's decision to terminate his sessions with Dr. Fourth. He said he no longer felt the need for therapy. Through a young man he had met at Sachs, he moved from the East Ninety-sixth Street area on the seething rim of Spanish Harlem into that heartland of rebellion, iconoclasm—and drug culture —known as the East Village. There, in the rear of a dreary, unkempt tenement, he acquired a two-room apartment.

More than six years later, in drafting a letter requesting

readmission to Harvard, not many weeks before his death, Michael was to write:

After a month or two of working, I took a small apartment of my own, on the outskirts of "Spanish Harlem," and proceeded to write and play the flute. Then I moved to the Lower East Side (199 Avenue B) where I really began, *for the first time in my life* [in his draft those words were underlined], to feel a sense of personal growth. My main interest at this point was studying the flute; this became more of a profession than a hobby; I was determined to be a great flutist, although I had only begun to play at college. But I also enjoyed the company of friends.

Yet even while Michael's dismissal of his therapist and his plunge into the heady atmosphere of the East Village could have been construed as a long advance from the gloom of the previous September, there were soon too many signs that his revived lust for life was precarious.

There was a resurgence of irrational compulsiveness, as when, after writing the memoir (which he did not show us), he decided that it should be published and consulted Nancy's parents about how to get this done. He actually sent it to at least one publisher—after the next breakdown, we found the letter of rejection in his desk.

In the same period, he proclaimed insistently that he wanted his new apartment completely and extensively furnished at once and, having failed to accumulate any substantial savings, he called on us to subsidize the whole venture. Dr. Fourth, with whom we had remained in contact, did not approve of our decision. She felt that it was time to compel Michael to display some realism about his own situation—and, in fact, his work at Sachs had begun to falter and deteriorate just as he was making rather lavish plans for his apartment.

Nevertheless we agreed to pay the bills, perhaps because we could not bear—or did not dare—to rebuff him at a moment when his eyes seemed to be dancing with the joy of living for the first time in so long. Was the decision consequential? Actually, as Michael was to see it, that spring was one of the few bright interludes in nearly a decade of illness. That the euphoria was self-deceptive did not detract from its temporary glow. How much of his pleasure may have been induced or sustained by the use of drugs, ultimately including LSD, is a question he was not then or even thereafter disposed to discuss. He preferred to savor the memory of a time, too brief, in which he felt he had tasted a rich, diverse existence too long denied him.

His career at Sachs, apparently so full of potential when it started, had ended in February.

As Dick Sachs recounts the deterioration:

Michael, after his promotion, showed considerable promise—quick to learn, bright, cooperative, perceptive—but a wavering self-confidence continued to make him unsure of himself.

Problems began to arise with Michael as he was asked to assume more responsibility in his work, make some relatively simple decisions, and face new challenges. According to the buyer for whom he worked, he seemed to tire easily and become distracted. On a few occasions, he was found playing the flute at his desk during his lunch hour when half the office was still working. When he was asked to stop, he would play in the men's room.

During this period I had two talks with Michael in an effort to help him develop a little better sense of himself in a business organization. What became increasingly frustrating to me, and perhaps to Michael, was that he so clearly had the ability to do outstanding work, but not the sense of purpose to let himself do it. I suggested to him at the time that I could understand his not finding business the most fascinating career but that the experience could be helpful to him. He agreed with me, said he felt a little foolish and would try to apply himself.

Our merchandise manager, who is the vice-president in charge of our buying office, is a man very sensitive to the disillusionment of young people. He talked with me about Michael on several occasions because he could see real talent and wanted to find a way to cut through some of Michael's disinterested facade and bring out the abilities he saw lurking beneath the surface.

We gave Michael a raise early in February, 1965, at the suggestion of the merchandise manager and personnel director. We felt it might convince Mike that we appreciated his work and could see some meaningful potential. The thought was that the recognition would help him to settle down and to realize that he could make progress on his own.

Unhappily, this experience was not Michael's cup of tea. There were too many people, the atmosphere was too hectic and overwhelming. It is a very fast track and Michael was not the first to be put off by it. Retailing requires people who don't mind working under pressure, meeting deadlines, keeping on schedule. It isn't for everyone. It wasn't for Michael.

Michael continued to be erratic in his work habits and very unsettled about what he was doing. It was about this time (mid-February, 1965) that I called reluctantly to discuss the problem with you.

You know the rest.

The rest was that Dick, sadly and painfully, felt obliged to call me with the warning that Michael was facing the prospect of discharge. It was agreed that there would be a final chance, but when I talked with Michael and transmitted the warning, his response was both defiant and evasive. At first, he denied that he was in trouble, then he sought to blame others for his predicament. But he could not challenge my reminder that Dick, who, after all, ran the place, was his friend and had sought at every turn to give him maximum opportunity for advancement.

If Michael had argued at that point, as he did later, that his real interests were elsewhere—creative, for example, rather than commercial—the conversation would have been less discouraging. But he had often expressed a yearning for a degree of financial success that would eventually guarantee his independence and security. Dick had made it plain that he regarded him as a bright prospect. After talking with Michael I had the dread that his failure at Sachs reflected the recurrence of familiar symptoms of breakdown rather than any thoughtful appraisal of alternatives.

Yet, after his job there was terminated, he did not appear to fall apart. He found a job at a rent-a-car agency. He also found a girl. She was shy, pleasant, several years younger, probably no more than seventeen.

The second job lasted only a month. Michael told us that he lost it because his employers were going out of business, but the explanation was somehow unconvincing. We rather suspected that he had found it an intrusion on his flute-playing and his private life. On an application for unemployment insurance he wrote in explanation of his job loss: "They could no longer use me."

He visited us infrequently but one evening in early spring he invited us to his apartment for dinner. It was crammed with burglar-detection devices, not to be considered paranoid on the rough street on which he lived. His young girl roommate was there, and they had diligently prepared a rather sumptuous steak dinner; Michael had also taken pains to provide our preferred brands of whiskey. He was in a warm, genial mood. He told us with satisfaction of a number of new friends he had made. He also disclosed that each Sunday morning, presumably at his companion's request, he was singing in the choir of a local church, perhaps the most astounding news of all in view of his record of disinterest in religious matters.

When we finished dinner he announced, without belligerence and indeed in his most appealing manner, that he had a proposal to present. He had decided that he wanted to dedicate himself to mastering the flute; he had been taking flute lessons and would now like to try to earn a living giving them, but he would need an allowance until he had established himself as a teacher and as a player.

Although Nancy had misgivings about the idea because she felt he had not demonstrated his qualifications for teaching, we went along. It must have been I who led the weak chorus of parental assent. But at that point there was, I think, a real difference between us. What moved me most that evening was a remark Michael made to me while the women were washing the dishes. Describing the joys of living that he had found in the East Village, he said he would always remember the happiness of the present, and that the memory would fortify him if he ever suffered a relapse. Never again, he said, would he contemplate self-destruction because he now knew what life could be like at its best.

When we left I told Nancy what he had said and how reassuring I found it. Her own recollection is that she was less relieved. The difference really involved perhaps my sentimental view that it mattered less whether Michael was showing some clear direction in life than whether he had begun to achieve a capacity for the enjoyment of living. Nancy, whose opinion was generally supported by the therapists we encountered, feared he would not attain any lasting stability until he proved he could organize his activities. She had no moral censure for his way of living, but she feared that, in view of his history, it would lead only to another cycle of disintegration.

What happened in the ensuing weeks deflated my hopes and vindicated her anxieties.

Michael, acting out his self-portrait as flute teacher, placed an ad in the *Village Voice* and printed an enormous number of cards in which he represented himself as capable of flute instruction "at all levels." He was unquestionably gifted, but he had virtually no formal musical training and was plainly unqualified to teach beyond any elementary level. He did find a couple of pupils, children of friends of ours. One of the parents told us Michael was proving a magnificent teacher for his young son; he was conscientious about keeping appointments with the boy for many weeks. But that was about the extent of his accomplishment in that role. Clearly the notion that he could support himself as a teacher was a delusion.

At the same time, he became preoccupied—perhaps the clinical word is *obsessed*—with a variety of get-rich-quick schemes and dreams that he wanted to patent. Some of them were quite inventive, but he abandoned them when he learned he would have to develop his formulae before seeking a patent. Then he turned to writing letters for information about all sorts of "selling" projects, but nothing came of that either.

One of his more grandiose visions, conceived not long after he moved to the East Village, was to build a harpsichord. But he soon decided that he could not execute that while holding a job (he still had one at that time) and asked us to agree to finance a helper. It was a rather absurd plea, but we agreed. What seemed to matter most was to prevent him from losing interest in things and returning to the shell of the previous September. He defended his erratic course by a somewhat persuasive insistence that he did not want to take a "boring" job. His projects, however, became increasingly grotesque and capricious, and there were renewed paranoiac symptoms.

One day in May he called Nancy at her office (he was coming home very seldom) to say that he and some friends wanted to start a coffee house. He wanted her to find out the legal requirements; there was about $1,500 that we had put aside for him and he was now thinking of investing it. He had friends who ran what they called a "Living Room" where he helped and where he was involved in playing music. If he put in the money, they would help him run the coffee house. While Nancy was getting the information on licensing and so forth, he hung around various coffee houses trying to learn about them. The two friends involved—a man named Chester and a woman named Wendy—did "therapy," he said, with young people in the East Village. He was helping them help these sick young people—the blind forever leading the blind. We later learned that both of these friends had histories of mental illness.

After Michael was hospitalized again, Nancy obtained some picture of that setup:

When I tried to clear out Mike's apartment and gather together his belongings, the harpsichord turned out to be in the "Living Room" and I went there to see about removing it. The "Living Room" was a storefront on an East Village slum street, one large room filled with mattresses and cots. Young people, most of them very young, lay on the cots in various states of torpor. No one said anything. Some of them looked at me; others seemed sightless. There was a young man in charge who agreed that I could come by with the moving men to take away the harpsichord. Wendy, with whom I spoke a number of times while making these arrangements, told me at great length how she and Chester were using LSD to help these troubled kids and how sorry she was that they hadn't been able to help Mike more! She did not explain her qualifications for this medical endeavor, but she pressed me to make financial contributions to the work. Later she called on the phone for the same purpose and even went to Jimmy's office.

After the coffee-house plan was broached, there followed a few weeks of phone calls back and forth, and Nancy made it clear to Michael that we were not prepared to hand over the $1,500 for the venture. He became steadily more insistent, irrational, and irritable about the project. Even his voice changed. As things got worse, it took on a strange, faraway quality; sometimes he would break off in the middle of a conversation and his words would fade off into the distance, like a train going across country. Our concern mounted and we told him so. One day he said that he had taken LSD, but that he had been in touch with

Dr. Third, who knew about it and told him it was "all right."

Nancy called Dr. Third, who confirmed that Mike had been in touch with him and had told him about taking LSD. Dr. Third said he thought this was dangerous and suggested we talk to Dr. Fourth. She agreed with Dr. Third's view, but felt there was little we could do. Michael saw her once more and she derived no reassurance from the session. We persuaded Mike to agree to come home for dinner one night and were shocked by his gaunt appearance and even more by his weird restlessness. He could hardly sit still; he had a recorder with him that he played almost constantly. When asked a question, he would often neglect to answer and tootle on the recorder instead.

In addition to his dissolute appearance and wild recorder playing, there was something alarming about his face—he was constantly grimacing. He left very early and we had no idea what to do; we were frightened and bewildered by what we had seen and heard. He had talked about how, when some unidentified East Villager behaved improperly toward "my girl," he put a billy in his belt and accosted the alleged offender on the street "just to scare him." He had other tales of incipient brawls, all of them wholly inconsistent with the distaste for violence that he had exhibited most of his life.

We implored him to resume therapy, despite all the sad evidence of its ineffectiveness, but he refused. And there were days —such as one when he came to my office for lunch—when he seemed momentarily cheerful. One evening, my mother reported, Michael had come by for dinner with my parents at their apartment in the West Village; in fact, she said, he had visited them twice in the same day. Her delight over his attentiveness—my father was by then an invalid—seemingly overshadowed any perplexity about his manner or his sudden interest.

Exactly when Michael first took LSD remains uncertain. But his involvement was clearly more extensive than he initially acknowledged. After his next hospitalization we were to find in his apartment an unmailed letter with the envelope addressed to Dr. Richard Alpert, Timothy Leary's LSD collaborator, that indicated that he had been in touch with him. It sounded as if he regarded himself as a fellow traveler of those who had committed themselves to the lifetime trip. The letter, dated May 19, read:

Dear Dr. A:

Since having talked at O'Henry's very good, if not wondrous things have happened.

Although they all have involved LSD (sugar cubes, "400 micrograms"), none of them have been that simple. However, especially because LSD was used, I'm a little worried lest my gains (emotional, musical, character, etc.) be transient. But, I'm very determined to keep them; it seems that all I need is courage (it isn't all that scary, after all!).

You're right—my "brain" *is* pretty damn interesting!

Although I have no desire, at this time, to join you (I do hope to come one Sunday, however)—I may, one day, desire such.

If so, I hope you'll consider me seriously. I now have a more realistic opinion of myself; it's quite possible I could be a useful and personable member of your community (e.g., see enclosed card).

Sincerely, Mike

P.S. Please keep all such communications of mine *within the community.*

The signs of decline multiplied. More and more, we were in the role of horrified but inert spectators watching someone we loved falter blindly toward the edge of a cliff.

Neither Dr. Third nor Dr. Fourth seemed disposed to intervene decisively. There was, of course, no way they could demand his presence, and our contacts with them diminished even as our helplessness grew. Finally Nancy called Dr. Liss to arrange another informal consultation. But on the night before the scheduled appointment we reached a crisis.

It was an evening in late May. Michael had invited Holly and the young man she later married, David Karpf, to his apartment for dinner, as he had done before. But when they arrived and rang the doorbell repeatedly, there was no response.

Nancy and I had dined out that night. When we got back to our apartment, David and Holly were there to tell us of their unsuccessful East Village expedition. It was agreed that Nancy would remain at home in case Michael called while David, Holly, and I took a cab downtown to see if we could find him.

Again there was no answer when we pressed his doorbell. We
wandered around a few neighboring streets and looked into bars
and coffee houses in our futile search.

Then, mystified and apprehensive, we rode back uptown. It
was a little before midnight when the phone rang, but the caller
was not Michael. It was one of his East Village friends who told
me urgently that I had better come down at once: "Mike is full
of LSD and the cops are all over his apartment."

At my request one of the policemen came to the phone. He
explained that Michael had been loudly and wildly playing his
flute, apparently in the hallways as well as in his own apartment, and that neighbors had registered angry complaints. I
asked him whether he could let Michael remain there until I arrived but he said that was impossible because of the clamor of
the tenants; he said it would be more advisable for us all to
meet at the East Third Street precinct.

When I reached there, I had only a brief chance to greet and
glimpse Michael—disheveled, pacing feverishly, but apparently
creating no disturbance at the moment—before the lieutenant in
charge invited me into his office. I instinctively anticipated a
stern encounter in which I would plead for mercy before the
hard visage of the law. Instead the lieutenant said very softly
that he understood the problem. "My sister's had a lot of trouble
with her kid," he explained. "She's going broke paying those
doctors." He did not want to press any charges against Michael,
but he could not let him go back to his apartment in view of the
temper of the tenants. He would, however, release him in my
custody if Michael agreed to go home with me at once. The alternative, he said, was to book him and then put him into the
Bellevue psychiatric ward. "I hate to send any kid to that hell-
hole," he said.

I thanked him warmly and explained these generous terms to
Michael. At first he appeared to consent: "Good deal!" But out
on the sidewalk as the police were trying to hail a cab for us,
Michael began to demur. "I might like to see what it's like at
Bellevue," he mumbled. Finally the cab was there and he
agreed to get in. When I gave the driver the address, Michael
immediately interjected that he wanted to be dropped off "at
the Waldorf." A friend of his was being married there, he kept
repeating.

The driver, of course, ignored him. Michael then shifted to the theme that we were being followed by FBI agents; he would turn around and point to various vehicles as bearers of G-men. When this seemingly interminable journey ended, Michael at first refused to leave the cab, insisting anew that the Waldorf was his destination. Finally the driver turned to him and shouted exasperatedly, with the immortal finality of New York cabbies: "Look, now you just get out of here and go upstairs with your father—I heard all the trouble you've been causing all the way up here."

Michael smiled almost whimsically and obediently followed the order.

When we got upstairs, David was just leaving. Nancy and I agreed that we could not wait until morning for medical help. We tried unsuccessfully to reach Dr. Fourth, who was still ostensibly the therapist in charge; she subsequently told us that she had disconnected her phone for the night. It was now about 2:00 A.M. Somewhat frantically, we telephoned Dr. R. the friend and psychiatrist whom we had known since our college days and with whose daughters Michael had had pleasant associations. He knew of Michael's problems and, when we explained that we were unable to reach Dr. Fourth, he volunteered to get up and come over at once.

This is how Holly remembers the interval after Michael and I arrived and before Dr. R. appeared:

When Mike came in the door he was highly excited and wild-eyed. He insisted that we all accompany him to "the Waldorf" to a friend's party. He was having intense visual experiences: I was wearing a rather nondescript black/brown/white bathrobe, but Michael kept marveling at the wonderful golden threads he professed to see in it. At first, Mike was just excited, but, as the night wore on, his manner became threatening, almost violent. My mother, father, and I were at a loss to handle the situation. Michael kept acting as if he would strike us. I could imagine the headlines: Son kills family and himself. I kept wondering how this could be happening to *my* family.

At one point I asked Mike to come with me to get a coke. As soon as we walked into the kitchen I regretted having done so—it occurred to me that we were standing next to a drawer of carving knives. I wanted to let my brother know how much I cared for him because I was afraid he might destroy himself before the evening was out. Before that, however, Michael had raised his hand as if to strike me but instead lowered his hand gently on my shoulder. I said, "I just want you to know that I love you." He answered softly, "I love you all too —perhaps too much."

After about an hour of this tension, I managed to escape into my room. I closed the door and dialed David's number. As soon as I reached him I started crying hysterically as I tried to explain the nightmarish scene. However, I had barely begun to tell David of the uproar when Michael threw open my door, asking why I had shut it, and, seeing the phone, grabbed the receiver from my hand. He said good-by to David and hung up. Then he told me to go back into the living room. Meanwhile my parents managed to reach their friend, Dr. R., who agreed to come over to speak to Mike. When the doorbell rang at 3:00 a.m., I answered it and said, "Oh, thank God you're here."

After the door closed behind Michael, my father, and Dr. R. on their way to the psychiatric ward of the hospital, my mother pulled me into her arms and I sobbed out my fear, fatigue, and desperation. As my tears began to ebb, I suddenly realized that not only was my mother comforting me, but I was holding a totally defeated, exhausted, and heartbroken woman in my arms, too. When the moment passed, Mother made us some tea and we sat in the living room and watched the sun's rays over the Hudson River.

It took Dr. R. only a few moments to decide that Michael required immediate hospitalization. Fortunately he was closely identified with Fairhope Hospital and quickly arranged by telephone for Michael's admission. (Our inability to reach Dr. Fourth had been a piece of luck; she told us later that she had no similar hospital connections.)

Michael was alternately truculent and mischievous as he entered the hospital. He began to insist that we had lured him there with the promise that we, or at least Dr. R., would remain with him. When he was offered sedatives, he threw them on the floor at Dr. R.'s feet. Whether LSD had any fundamental bearing on Michael's breakdown or had merely triggered an inevitability must be added to the list of many questions for which therapists provided no answers.

I tried to put my arm around Michael as Dr. R. and I were leaving. He pushed it aside, renewing the accusation that our departure was a betrayal. Although the hospital is judged a splendid place among medical institutions, I had begun to learn a little of what it must be like to walk into the open air and leave a son behind in prison. Yet it is also true, in Nancy's words, that on that morning "we could only feel relief that Michael was somewhere where he could be taken care of."

IX

A Time of Nothingness

THE HOSPITAL to which Michael had been taken did not provide long-range therapy, perhaps fortunately, because its fees were immense. Almost from the time Michael entered, a major subject of discussion was where he would be placed after he had exhausted the three-month time limit there, or even before.

One puzzling aspect of this hospital's procedure was the absence of any bridge between its doctors and those who had hitherto treated Michael. But we had encountered this form of psychiatric "isolationism" before and we would face it again. Whatever the merits of the theory that each therapist should start afresh, presumably unhampered by the misconceptions of earlier men, a sad consequence was the requirement that Michael rehearse the details of his life so often before so many different audiences of one, and, in a few instances, before panels of onlookers. It must also be said that it was our experience, with infrequent exceptions, that psychiatrists rarely exhibit any reverence for each other's opinions even when they profess to be cooperating.

Another phase of the hospital world we were now to learn more about (we had seen it to some degree at Pleasant View) was the extent to which patients were the primary province of "residents," rather than of the senior psychiatrists who supervised the wards. In some situations, a young resident may prove more flexible and imaginative than an older doctor. But when a patient has already been in the hands of four seasoned therapists, as Michael had been, he may tend, as Michael did, to view himself as more sophisticated than the young man assigned to him. The young resident was the only psychiatrist we saw at Fairhope. Although there was a senior psychiatrist who supervised the ward, we never met him.

In his first weeks there Michael was still quite "psychotic"; we put quotations marks around the word because so many of the definitions became more rather than less obscure as we tried to understand what the doctors were saying. A cruder description would be "out of his mind," in the sense that there was neither coherence nor intelligibility in much that he said or wrote. When Nancy first visited him after the long night, he greeted her as "Mrs. Wechsler." Later, he was to divulge to his doctor that he was convinced she was an FBI agent. He was constantly accompanied by a nurse.

Gradually he was calmer, established friendships with other patients, especially young women, and began to participate in dances, occupational therapy, and other activities. But the young resident told us that the staff's conclusion was that long-term hospitalization was essential, perhaps as much as two years. The only diagnosis they communicated to us was that he was "quite sick." While Michael seemed reconciled to the prospect of transfer, he was talking about another brief time out to be followed by a return to Harvard.

In our discussions the resident said the staff recommended Brightlawn as the hospital where a young man in Michael's condition would be most likely to overcome his illness. It had, he said, a "special program" for youthful patients, but the details were not explained.

To us Brightlawn had the threatening sound of a large, catchall state institution; we felt we owed Michael something better and began to explore other possibilities. It was surprising to discover in this quest how many practicing psychiatrists not only had no formal relationships with hospitals (as Dr. Fourth had acknowledged) but knew very little about most of the institutions mentioned to us. Our inquiries about private hospitals indicated that several of them had solid reputations, but so had Pleasant View, from which Michael had apparently derived no benefit during the summer of 1964. Moreover, most of them were distant from the city; the cost of maintaining a patient at one of those most frequently suggested was between $25,000 and $35,-000 a year.

As we pursued this inquiry, we heard many favorable comments about another state hospital that had the incidental but appealing advantage of being located in the borough in which we lived. When we proposed it to the resident, his response was enthusiastic but he warned that it was extremely difficult to gain admission. Its prestige, however, was a major asset in convincing Michael of its desirability—he, too, had heard respectful comment about it through the patient grapevine. With his acquiescence assured, we exerted all available influence and we hailed the news that he had been accepted with some of the same delight we had felt when Harvard opened its doors to him.

In the ambulance on the way to Statewide from Fairhope, I said to Michael—and I believed it—that this time we were going to the right place at the right time and this time he would finally make it. And he nodded, with that smile Dr. Liss had called "beatific." Michael assured me that he would do everything he could to take advantage of the opportunities that Statewide would offer. He promised to be a highly cooperative patient.

One curious contretemps accompanied the transfer. In contrast with the pattern to which we have referred, Statewide actively solicited written information and guidance from therapists who had previously treated its new patients. We were astounded to hear that Dr. First had refused to answer any questionnaires or, in fact, "put anything in writing." Finally, after much discussion, he said he would be willing to give oral replies to certain questions. The episode revived earlier antagonisms and made things even more difficult when he later reentered the case.

Ironically, the day on which Michael went to Statewide was that July day on which President Johnson announced the escalation of the Vietnam war. When we picked him up at Fairhope, nearly all the patients were assembled listening to the speech. Michael was quite agitated, declaring that Mr. Johnson was at least as "crazy" as he and his fellow patients. (We were to be struck by how often, in years of hospitalization, Michael and others were to comment with asperity on the mental condition of those directing the war.)

Michael remained at Statewide for slightly more than a year —July, 1965, to August, 1966. In that period he managed to run away from the hospital eight times—*elope* was the lingo for such escape—and that was how he finally ended his tenure there. By the time of his last flight, it was clear to us and those whom we consulted that there was nothing to be gained from his remaining there.

Statewide, like Fairhope, was a "teaching hospital"; nearly all of the treatment was conducted by young residents. (This, of course, is significantly more than most public hospitals offer; in a large majority there is no individual therapy.) Statewide's director told us with some pride that his institution got "the cream of the crop" of medical school graduates, and no doubt it did.

Soon after Michael entered, we received an unexpected phone call from the director. He wanted to know whether we preferred to have Michael placed in the hands of a new MD resident or of a woman who lacked a medical degree but possessed several years of clinical experience at another hospital. It had not occurred to us that our opinion would (or should) be solicited on this selection—we felt no competence about choosing between strangers. We had the uneasy sense that the invitation was a concession to my journalistic status, as if, alas, this freedom of choice would enhance the view that there was something very special about Statewide.

After some reflection, we agreed on the woman, perhaps still influenced by Dr. Third's notion that Michael had reached the point at which a woman therapist could work most effectively with him.

Both at Fairhope and in his early weeks at Statewide Michael was feverishly typing poetry. Like many of his drawings, much of it was a mixture of cleverness and mindlessness, sadness and madness—but who is to draw the line? Some excerpts:

> Such beautiful youthful truthful
> Independence of a young country.
> Banners, bubbles, and animals'
> Troubles, waving in the wind
> like the mane of a bountiful pony,
> so baffled by her brazenly
> wonderlanded bubbly bunny
> Ways.

> ! ! !

A *Better Poem*

After all—what follows that fourth of
July exuberance can only be exonerated
as something more mature, from a more
stable and truthful mind. . . .
Besides, the ugly, frightened,
uncertain other part of a Spring-wind-
blown mind would, mature or not, blow
my . . . mind completely! Mines to a mind.
And more power to us all!

To this he appended the handwritten observation: "Yup. Very
seriously (seriously!) psychotic at this point (chuckle)."

Forgotten

Oh hateful angry jealous
lover—
why hast thou forsaken me,
little me, who had no more
and no worse than the best
of the worst intentions!

August 11, 1965

Untitled

Where paradoxes rain, and
dogs and cats fly upward;
The ones who are insane will
still strive forward.
Starward, bar-ward, car-ward
tarred and feathered by their own
minds. To find just a little
level crammed with goodies of
peace on this earth and good will
to these men and women Now!
Oh God, why hast thou forsaken all
us mad people who prayed again and
then once more; what other than madness
is in store. What More!
There must be a Brave New World's
private island for deprivated minds.
Distraction leads to more interaction
from one diseased brain to the next.

Get rid of our tortured different all
seeing and nothing knowing minds.
Peace on this earth, and goodwill
to us; that's our only true prayer,
oh omniscience. Oh Jean Paul Sartre—
that is your name, isn't it? Who
really feels that "existential" Dread?
I do, and you haven't had enough to
become mad, and sad for ages and ages
And pages and pages of many a lying
text. Freud, you, in your later years,
would have been locked up and driven
to more madness if your insight came
just a few decades later. Where
are we now, Freud. In Vietnam? Yes!
In Mad Places? Still! Kill with frills,
they shall still. Blow up, die, disaster,
curtains to all our minds.
Look! Listen! Harken All!
That's all my all is for.

Statewide was physically comfortable, clean, staffed by people who seemed generally able and dedicated. Michael's therapist was a warm, communicative woman whom he saw two or three half-hours each week.

When Michael first entered Statewide, he was still somewhat agitated, but the turbulent psychosis had passed. Although he seemed to agree to the move, by the time he had been there a few days he changed his mind; he said he wanted to get out and return to Harvard. The initial drive to leave tapered off, but within five to six weeks he eloped for the first time. His therapist, Dr. Fifth, was very conscientious, but this was a period of constant battle. Michael was running away periodically; he was objecting to the medication on which the hospital insisted. Dr. Fifth diagnosed him as "impulsive" and "defiant" and said these characteristics would have to come under control before therapy could be productive. The hospital authorities thought Michael could not make progress until he accepted a rationale for being there. Instead, however, he persisted in eloping. After a number of such flights, the hospital said he would be expelled unless we agreed to a sixty-day commitment. In part they wanted the

legal authority to make him stay; in part they wanted us to con-
vey unequivocally to Michael that we were not going to help
him run away. Each time he eloped this was the issue, and Michael knew that Nancy and I were not in full agreement between ourselves about the wisdom—or necessity—of bringing
him back to the hospital.

There was an earnest effort to involve parents (nearly all the
patients in Michael's ward were young). We saw the therapist
on several occasions, and there was a program of weekly interviews with a social worker who was supposed to serve as inter-
locutor between family and therapist. Later there were gatherings at which all five of us were present, but the social worker
was supposed to be the link between patient and parents.

Unfortunately the systematic sessions with Miss Gee, the social worker, seemed increasingly aimless to me (and, to a lesser
extent, to Nancy).

In the times when we met with Miss Gee alone she invariably began the session by saying: "How do you feel?"

After one of those encounters I remember saying to Nancy
on our way home: "Someday I'm going to tell her 'I feel absolutely fine because it's so nice to drive up here and see my son
miserable and apparently making no progress.'" But we agreed
that Miss Gee was earnestly performing a ritual dictated by the
hospital and that our response to the question was supposed to
be in some fashion revealing, although it usually took the form
of a grunt or grimace.

Eventually, when the therapist, social worker, and Michael
were all present, one of them boldly advanced the subject of Michael's confession that he was sexually drawn to Nancy. Miss
Gee looked at me and asked me how I felt about this disclosure.

I responded too glibly, "I think it shows he has very good
taste." She and the therapist laughed and indicated they regarded this response as a gem of wit and generosity. I looked at
Michael and saw that he had been hurt by the frivolity, perhaps
even by a sense that I had somehow managed to "steal the
show." I stumbled into a labored discourse of my familiarity
with *Oedipus Rex*, suggesting my sophisticated awareness that
there was obviously nothing remotely new or consequential
about this problem and compounding the injury with each

word. But presumably such exchanges were vital for Miss Gee's notebooks and she had been, like so many others before and after, acting out of genuine concern as well as adhering to the form-charts. My mother would have said, quite justly, "She means well."

What rendered our meetings with Miss Gee so dispiriting—and intensified my ill-concealed impatience about them—was that she had so little news to report. On October 16, 1965, I visited Michael on his twenty-third birthday (at that point he was permitted to see only one of us at a time). He tried to react amiably to the gifts I had brought, but nothing could make this a cheerful occasion. He had become steadily more depressed by the passage of time and the knowledge that he had made no headway in dealing with the world or himself. His inability to return to Harvard to obtain his degree was a frustrating source of discontent and was to remain to him a symbol of failure as late as the last week of his life. He appeared convinced that Statewide's reputation was a fraud, and much of his time was devoted to plotting flight.

It was less than two months after his arrival that he engineered his first successful break. He reached our door in early morning, vowing he would not go back, at least not immediately. We called the hospital and the officials insisted on his return. After a day of wrangling, exhortation, and pleading on our part, he capitulated. But this was to be only the first of what he later reported, with some pride, had become recognized as a record series of unauthorized departures.

Whether patients got weekend passes at Statewide depended on their therapist; the decisions were communicated by the social worker. There was not supposed to be any direct communication between the family and his therapist, Dr. Fifth, except as arranged by the social worker. This broke down in periods of crisis, which soon became almost continuous because of Michael's repeated runaways.

One of them was especially astounding. It occurred during one of the many intervals when he was required to remain in pajamas by day as well as night; patients not deemed eligible for passes were not supposed to dress in street clothes. Nevertheless, he had somehow eluded the guards, taken a subway, and made it home. It is perhaps a small footnote to the annals of modern New York as well as of Statewide that a bearded young man—by that time he had grown a full, bushy one—could wander into the streets attired in a robe and pajamas without apparently evoking any notice or interception. But the hospital said Michael was the only patient who had achieved the distinction of escape while thus attired.

There was a small storm over this episode because it developed that the hospital was unaware of his absence until we telephoned to report that he was with us. We suggested rather vehemently to the therapist and social worker that there was some flaw in their security system; they were deeply embarrassed by what they described as an inexplicable lapse.

As the exits and reentrances continued, it became steadily harder for me to get into the spirit of admonishing Michael to return there. But Nancy realistically and resolutely kept pointing out that there was no alternative; clearly Michael was not in condition to be on his own, even if he were to live with us.

The hospital's view was that when a patient was progressing he would demonstrate his improvement by taking a job or enrolling in school and gradually showing a capacity to manage on his own; one step was to follow another. As the patient showed what he could do, his privileges would be increased, enabling him to spend more and more time out of the hospital. Some patients did no more than sleep at the hospital and went to school or jobs during the day. Michael refused to accept the need to "earn" his way out. He wanted to skip the intervening steps and obtain the privileges when he thought he was ready. For weeks he struggled tenaciously to secure them without going through the required preliminaries. In time he got his way and was allowed to be absent from the hospital part of each day, although he was not supposed to come home to us. We gathered that he spent his time aimlessly wandering around, taking pictures, picking up girls for brief flirtations. Finally the hospital plausibly decided that this drifting was unsatisfactory but agreed to give him a "last chance."

Both of us were dismayed and disheartened by what we saw on our visits. Michael was listless and drowsy. He complained about the heavy dosages of Thorazine he was receiving; sometimes he flared up explosively in protesting the sedation. The tranquilizer seemed to be not only transforming him into a sleepwalker; it was causing him to gain weight. His clothes, when he was allowed to wear them, ceased to fit and required replacement. Michael protested that he no longer needed pacification, and certainly not in such large doses. The hospital officials were adamant about prescribing it. That argument dragged on for several months.

Finally, in triumphant confirmation of his point, Michael confessed that for many weeks he had not been swallowing the dose handed out to him. The hospital staff conceded that it had not noticed anything troublesome about his behavior during this period and belatedly agreed to reduce the medication.

This extraordinary incident heightened my doubts about this psychiatric island, and I began to express reluctance about "imprisoning" Michael much longer. How dull or inattentive could this celebrated establishment be if Michael had, in effect, been able to contrive this ruse to stop the excessive Thorazine? The social worker began to reproach me for my lack of faith. There were allegations that my transparent skepticism about Statewide's formulae was infecting Michael and partially responsible for the sluggishness of his response to therapy. Floundering as we were, I tried to improve my deportment. Thus, after one of Michael's elopements, when the hospital demanded that he sign a twenty-five-day self-commitment paper, I joined in successfully urging him to do so. On January 24, 1966, despite my own misgivings, I wrote him:

Just a note to tell you that Miss Gee informed us of your decision regarding the twenty-five-day document. We think it was a wise one and hope that you feel the same.

As I have been meaning to write you for some days, I hope you realize that Mother and I devote a lot of thought to this problem; but everyone in whom we have confidence, and who cares about you, expresses great faith in Statewide, in the people there, and the results they have seen achieved. Dr. R. was over the other night and strongly affirmed that opinion.

I know that each day may seem an eternity; I can only urge you to remember that one day this period will seem a very small fragment of your life, and that it could mean a lot to your future. . . .

And again on February 10:

We continue to look forward to seeing you whenever you feel it is
indicated; we hope that you are finding things to do to make life less
dull than you have described it. . . .

But Michael was hardly inspired by such cheerleading. He
had heard it too often before, and his doubts were unrelieved by
verbal promissory notes.

We were getting nowhere, although Michael was more active and had developed friendships with other patients and with
some of the nurses. He brushed aside suggestions that he take
paying jobs inside the hospital; he rarely participated in organized patient activities. Finally, at some point in late spring, the
hospital spokesmen began to intimate that he was not "treata-
ble" there. They finally presented a plan under which he would
find a daytime job on the outside but sleep at the hospital each
night. Soon a part-time position was found for him at a photographer's studio.

Then, one weekend, when he was legally home on a pass,
Nancy arrived and found him shaving off the heavy beard that
he had grown at the hospital. This seemed a good omen. It was,
in fact, the start of a time when he seemed to be emerging from
that cycle of depression and aggression. We gained additional
hope when, having won his fight to halt heavy medication, he
began to lose weight and express some pleasure about the discovery that he was able to go to his part-time job in his old
clothes. Once again we thought he might be on his way back to
life.

Perhaps if there had been a continuity of therapists, he
might have been able to stay with the hospital treatment long
enough to achieve real gains. Perhaps that was another one of
our futile longings. Nevertheless, the startling thing was the
apparent survival or renewal of his resistance to disintegration.

Any prospect of decisive improvement was shadowed by Michael's realization that his therapist's one-year assignment at the
hospital was nearing an end. Despite the absence of any marked
recovery beyond the virtual disappearance of psychotic manifestations, he had obviously acquired an attachment for her. Now,

in his view, he would be starting all over again. The new therapist assigned to him—there was to be a certain overlapping during the transition—was an attractive, eager young man with little clinical background. After more than five years in the
psychiatric wilderness, Michael was again inclined to look at a
doctor as a brash pupil rather than potential savior. Very soon
after the change, Michael eloped from Statewide for the last
time.

As I have indicated, most of Michael's time at Statewide
seems to have been a fight to get out at any cost. He was consis-
tently hostile to rules and regulations. Dr. Fifth referred to his
intransigence as a basic personality trait, but that was not what
his personality had been before the illness. How did one differ-
entiate the "basic" character from the manifestations of sickness?
Those months were a continuing struggle to induce him to accept the need to concentrate on trying to get well rather than to
be absorbed with plans for running away. It was an unsuccessful battle. Perhaps that was inevitable; yet it was not that way
with many of the patients, and we have never known why Michael was so intractable. During much of this time, there recurred a tendency to argue that a therapist other than the one
in charge could do better, a point on which we often agreed; the
question always was, who could do better? While he was at
Statewide, Michael often said that the reason he wanted to
leave the hospital was his desire to be treated anew by Dr.
First. Although Dr. Third had been his doctor for the longest
time, and Dr. Fourth most recently, it was Dr. First to whom he
kept reverting in his darkest hours.

One of the patients with whom he became friendly was a
teller of tall tales who came to dinner one night and unfolded
wildly imaginative stories of adventures he allegedly had when
hitchhiking around the country. It was clear that this was an inventive fellow, but Mike accepted it all quite literally; he was
unwilling to be skeptical about anything this boy told him. Before his illness, Mike would have had no difficulty recognizing
the web of fantasy. Another friend was a very pretty girl who
had previously shown no impulse to elope. Mike got into trouble at the hospital by trying to encourage her to flee. This was

another aspect of the sharp change that had occurred in his personality. At Statewide Mike was unmistakably and rather proudly a troublemaker, unlike the good citizen he had been at school and the very reliable companion known to his family.

When Michael came home on weekends, he increasingly preferred to head for the West Village. After he was able to go out on passes alone he did go there—against Dr. Fifth's orders. One evening he came home for dinner with a rather attractive girl whom he had picked up in a coffee house. We still have photographs he took of her.

One Saturday night we accompanied him on his journey, wading through the throngs of kids on MacDougal Street. We sat with him in a coffee house surrounded by the rising Village generation of hippies—many very young, intense, rather sad. At that point coffee houses and the Village milieu symbolized the good life to Michael.

If the weekend was in the country he would ask us to take him to the local ice-cream parlor, where he would eat enormous banana splits and rather forlornly watch the carefree local kids on their dates.

It was shortly after the departure of Dr. Fifth from Statewide and the advent of his new therapist there that Michael decided to bolt. This time it was really farewell.

Instead of reporting at his daytime job, he cleaned out a small bank account still in his possession and headed for Cambridge, where his closest and oldest friend, Dave Robbins, had an apartment and where Holly and David Karpf were attending summer school. Holly well remembers Michael's arrival and the subsequent fortnight of his encampment:

One midafternoon in Cambridge, a girl I did not know but who lived in my dormitory knocked at my door. "Your brother is downstairs," she said. (Men were not allowed in the dorms.) I could not imagine how Michael had managed to make so fantastic an escape all the way to Harvard, but I hurried down to see for myself. When I saw Mike, I felt a mixture of things—part of the good part of my summer was the fact that I had escaped the tensions and sadnesses of a home which revolved around this lost, sad individual. And yet I deeply valued the closeness that my brother and I had begun to develop. I kissed him hello and inquired about the miracle of his newest elopement. I must say I must have encouraged this behavior because I was always fascinated to hear of his outwitting the hospital staff. Even as a young psychologist, I have little use for mental institutions and to this day I marvel at Michael's inventive escapes.

My first thought, however, was that my family must be frantic with worry. I persuaded Mike to call Dad. As it turned out, our parents did not yet know Mike was missing.

The two weeks that Mike spent in Cambridge were weeks of great conflict for me. Keeping track of my brother consisted of being constantly at his beck and call. This was partly because men were not allowed in the dorms and so, whenever Mike appeared, I had to go out for walks with him. I resented his demands and the daily phone calls from my father asking for reports on Michael's behavior. Mike's demeanor during this period was quite manic; he was agitated and restless and it was painfully difficult to relax with him or around him.

But it was not all grim. The first afternoon Mike was there he picked up a Radcliffe girl. She was a bit strange, and that night Michael, the girl, David Karpf, David Robbins, and I went out to a local coffee house to see an entertainer named "Howlin" Wolf. Suddenly Mike turned to the girl, smiled devilishly, and said, "By the way, I escaped from a mental hospital today." The girl laughed, but her laughter became nervous tittering when I assured her that Michael had indeed done just that. Mike enjoyed his confession and we all mischievously enjoyed making the girl uneasy.

The Cambridge excursion was something of a spree. Michael was smoking a lot of pot and, we gathered, was frenetically making dates with girls. We did persuade him to check in with Dr. Third, but there was no effort to resume therapy. While Dr. Third was conscientious about keeping track of Michael, he seemed as baffled as we were about what the next steps should be.

Having exhausted his money, and perhaps the patience of his host, Michael came back to our summer place in Westport. Where would he go from there? Nearly thirteen months at Statewide could be written off as largely wasted. It was now more than eight years since he had pronounced himself in need of psychiatric aid and soon he would be twenty-five or, as he put it morosely, "I'll soon have been alive for nearly a quarter of a century." He was no longer manic but seemed to be slipping back into depression.

We found ourselves once again turning to Dr. Liss, who now finally agreed that it might be desirable for him to talk to Michael directly.

At this point Michael was living on a low, spiritless level, involved in nothing, still expressing vague hope of a recovery sufficient to enable him to complete his Harvard studies, but engaged in no activity except some desultory flute-playing. But he doggedly used the sessions with Dr. Liss to argue his case for renewal of his therapeutic relationship with Dr. First.

We had long feared this development. Michael had become seemingly reconciled to the gap between Dr. First and myself, and he had only occasionally referred to him during and between his hospitalization. By then I had made clear, with Nancy's assent, that we would not finance any further treatment with Dr. First. Justly or not, we felt that he had been less than helpful and that he had tended to exploit and exacerbate adversary situations between Michael and ourselves. We had a growing conviction that he relieved his own insecurities by engaging in a kind of gamesmanship. We had long ago lost confidence in him, and he was perceptive enough to know it. Beyond that, I was increasingly convinced that his initial assessment of Michael's condition, especially his forecast of the possible need for a lifetime of therapy, had made it far more difficult for his successors, especially Dr. Second, to overcome Michael's dread that he was the victim of malignancy.

But Michael won the argument with Dr. Liss, persuading him that he believed that only Dr. First could help him at this juncture. We bowed to Liss's judgment that Michael should be given the chance to work with Dr. First again.

There followed an interminable interval of uncertainty. The time was August and Dr. First was not easy to find. Dr. Liss had volunteered to act as intermediary. Day after day, he reported that he had vainly tried to locate Dr. First; it began to assume the dimensions of a mystery story and it became harder each night to tell Michael that the search was still unsuccessful.

But at last contact was made. Dr. First told Dr. Liss he was extremely reluctant to resume his role as Michael's therapist. At Dr. Liss's suggestion, I telephoned Dr. First. He was aloof and negative, despite my obsequious entreaties, and finally I exclaimed, "Will you take Michael back if I crawl from my office to yours?" The conversation was narrowly salvaged, and Dr. First consented to see Nancy and me a few days later.

He told us at the start that he considered both of us hostile and uncooperative. (We refrained from reminding him of how stupidly cooperative we had been about buying the Volkswagen, or, indeed, about his refusal to meet us before he became Michael's therapist.) Nevertheless, his affection for Michael, he said, induced him to begin seeing him again, but he would do so only if he could bring a senior colleague into the case as a consultant. Dr. First said that he wanted to be backed up by another physician and also that he wanted someone with hospital connections, since the need for renewed confinement had to be anticipated.

We agreed unconditionally to all his terms. We promised to try to be more "cooperative," whatever that entailed. We assured him that we deemed his efforts indispensable to Michael. Dr. Liss, on whose gentle, selfless counsel we had relied so long, rationalized our deceit. If he could offer no better course at the time and we could think of none, our duty to Michael was clear. It turned out that Dr. Liss did not have many more months to live; perhaps some intimation of his own mortality prompted him to establish some therapeutic setting for Michael as quickly as possible. He may also have been comforted by the enlistment in a consultant capacity of the man who will be known as Dr. Sixth. Dr. Sixth was a man of his own generation and a figure of some renown in the profession, especially celebrated for his explorations of suicide.

Michael was visibly pleased; he still felt passionately that Dr. First could help him. During his deterioration in the East Village, he had apparently made overtures to regain him as his therapist. Dr. First had demanded some sort of letter from us, which he and Michael presumably knew we were not prepared to sign. In a long, chaotic, and unmailed note we found in that apartment after he was hospitalized, he wrote Dr. First:

I think I see what you were worried about when you requested a letter from my parents.

At any rate I have been (self-consciously for the most part) paranoid, as you may or may not know from having once spoken to Dr. Third.

I just wanted to let you know: among an infinitude of things I have learned, I have learned how and whom to trust. . . . It's easy to tell, in fact! The only question is how *much* to trust which people.

Of course that question applies to you (as, in fact, even to my "best" friends). Nevertheless you were (are) the best doctor in the sense of being least secured, i.e., you were least "likely to kill" yourself or me. (Witness: long weekends at your summer place.)

Frankly, if this letter sounds odd, I'd like to know. I want advice on a book I'm beginning; the subject is "communication." I am concerned mainly with "schizophrenic" communication. It may be the most dangerous kind but it also seems to be the most honest. There are many ramifications in these communications although workers (even doctors) and, I suppose, most schizophrenics have a pretty good idea about them (the communications).

If it sounds to you that I am wrapped up in grandiose paranoid delusions, let me say only . . . most of them *are* grand, even if they talk around the "point" a little.

Many regards, Mike

We assume this was written shortly before the night of the police episodes and during the LSD phase, but the letter was undated.

In the autumn, after the tortuous negotiations had been completed, Michael's sessions with Dr. First were resumed. Not long after they got under way, Nancy spent fifty minutes with Dr. First alone.

"I hoped to be able to talk out some of the misunderstandings of the past," she recalls. "But this was not possible because for forty-five of the fifty minutes Dr. First made a speech in which he detailed at length all of his grievances against us. When it was over there was nothing to do except hope that Mike was right and that Dr. First could help him."

Again I had a sense of how utterly entrapped we were by Michael's almost mystical faith in Dr. First and the initial misjudgment I had made in accepting the presence of a therapist with whom combat had been almost instinctive from the start. The question is not whether one of us was right or wrong; it was the doomsday quality of an adversary relationship that should have been frankly faced—and severed—before its long-range consequences became irremediable.

Throughout that fall and early winter Michael's life was empty and shapeless. His visits to Dr. First were his only formal activity. He remained in the apartment much of the time, playing the flute or recorder or listening to music in his room, rarely seeing either old school friends or alumni of the hospitals in which he had been. Occasionally he took solitary walks and, once in a while, journeyed to Village coffee houses ostensibly in search of companionship. Dr. First was successful in persuading him to avoid reinvolvement in drugs and to avoid a return to his East Village routine.

Holly, still living at home (she was married the following summer), began conscientiously trying to arrange dates for Michael, but he was awkward and withdrawn. He was uncomfortable when we had guests and avoided encounters with his grandparents and other relatives.

Then, in January of 1967, Holly brought him together with Betty. She had plotted this rendezvous with Mrs. Jones, one of her psychology teachers, with whom she had often discussed Michael. The teacher had long been a friend of Betty's family and was concerned about enhancing her social life. Betty, too, had experienced some emotional difficulties—but none approaching the dimensions of Michael's or requiring hospitalization. She was a handsome, robust, spirited young teacher to whom Michael appeared quickly drawn, and all of us were cheered by her advent.

Up until this point in his life Michael had had varying relationships with numerous girls. In Cambridge there were a few with whom he had gone to bed, one of them, according to his chronicles, an especially startling and temporarily gratifying nymphomaniac, but none of these liaisons lasted long or had any serious romantic overtones. By that time, if not earlier, Michael was plainly beginning to shrink from anything that signified involvement. Finally there had been the young girl with whom he had lived for a couple of months in the East Village, but this too seemed more a matter of convenience than a durable affair.

There were strikingly different notes in his alliance with Betty: At moments they seemed a truly devoted pair who had providentially found each other. One evening, when we were all together, Michael gaily said to Holly, "When am I going to meet that Mrs. Jones who arranged this mismatch?" He and Betty were affectionately holding hands, and a visitor might have described him as a lighthearted young man joyously and spontaneously falling in love.

Things were never quite that easy, but it had been a very long time since Michael had shown any comparable animation. Through much of the darkness, I had clung to a rather simplistic, romantic hope that Michael would find his way back to life through what used to be called "the love of a good woman" rather than on a psychiatrist's couch. With each failure of therapist and hospitalizations, that became an almost obsessive fantasy. Holly shared it and, the more we saw of Michael and Betty together, even Nancy, who was more skeptical, was touched by the contagion of the idea.

That is not to say that Michael seemed suddenly "cured." He did not. There was still much aloofness and edginess. Except for Betty, he led a largely unfocused existence although there were occasional signs of involvement in the outside world, such as participation in the Peace March of April, 1967. He was still dependent on us, a condition that alternately depressed and exasperated him.

Even in the best time that late winter and spring, we detected uneasy, uneven moments. Yet there were positive indications; Michael still had no occupation, but he had begun to move. He and Betty took bicycle rides in the park together and went to movies over the weekend. During the week Michael often spent his evenings at her nearby apartment and she frequently visited with us after which they would retire to his room. (Unfortunately, several "rough" streets had to be traversed and Michael was excessively nervous about the walking distance. But Betty deprecated his fears and helped to minimize them.)

The important thing was that Michael's lonely, empty existence throughout the autumn seemed to have been replaced by an authentic human involvement. What we did not learn until later was that Dr. First had a wholly different, negative view of the love story in which we had begun to find so much relief and invest so much hope.

X

From Betty to Brightlawn

EARLY THAT SPRING Nancy and I met with Dr. First and his
senior consultant, Dr. Sixth, at the latter's office. It was a period
when we heard the lovely sound of Michael whistling at breakfast in the morning and when it seemed possible to talk once
again about his future in the real world.

So now we were gathered, or so it seemed, to celebrate progress and discuss how to consolidate the gains. Although Dr.
First had heretofore counseled against "pushing" Michael, he
was now ready to discuss the next steps.

But before we got very far a disturbing colloquy occurred. I
had said I thought much of Michael's new demeanor was attrib-
utable to his relationship with Betty and that I felt an immense
gratitude toward her. Instantly Dr. First interposed, "It's not
Betty. It's what I've done."

Dr. Sixth, Nancy, and I glanced at each other almost fur-
tively, silently consenting not to dispute the allocation of cred-
its. Instead, I said with probably unconvincing cordiality that I
was indebted to both men for their continued attentiveness and
hoped it was unnecessary for us to debate the importance of
Betty's role.

Now, as so many years earlier, Dr. First had seemingly felt
some compulsion to prove something to us, or to himself. Worse
than that, he must have known that we construed his words as
an expression of jealousy toward a young woman who was in
love with Michael and with whom he was achieving at least
some respite from the years of desolate drift.

After Dr. First left, I could not resist calling attention again
to his curious remark about Betty. Dr. Sixth cautiously indicated
that it had troubled him, too, but urged us not to take it too seriously. What mattered was that Michael had apparently found

someone whose presence broke the monotony of "nothingness."

Later we were to find out that Dr. First not only disparaged the value of Betty's companionship; according to Betty, he had actively tried to discourage it and Michael had recurrently transmitted the news to her. Each time it was some variant of the phrase: "She's not good for you."

We can hardly appraise whether Dr. First's hostility affected the tragic sequel. There were tensions between Michael and Betty long hidden from us. In part, they centered on her unwillingness to have intercourse with him until there was some assurance that they would have a lasting and stable relationship. (This seemed less a demand for marriage than an expression of fear that his emotions were still quixotic.)

Michael's condition obviously affected his ability to give Betty the serenity she would need if they were to stay together. And while Dr. First was seemingly encouraging Michael to avoid the involvement, Mrs. Jones was aggressively sponsoring it. To some extent Michael and Betty were caught in an adult cross fire that made both of them distrust the glow of their brightest moments with each other.

Suddenly everything went wrong again.

Through the winter Michael had once more regained hope that he could return to Harvard the following autumn. Earlier he had made an effort to obtain admission to Columbia as a transfer student. The Columbia admissions authorities were not encouraging. Somehow, to Michael, completion of his undergraduate career remained his yardstick of recovery, the critical test of his conquest of those "morning fears."

That spring Michael went so far as to arrange for interviews in Cambridge about the possibility of readmission. In the process of preparing his brief for readmission, he wrote:

I have had many thoughts about returning to school. There has been a good deal of time to consider where it was all leading, and what some of the possibilities are. I do not want to return to school just because a college degree can be helpful in a practical way; at the same time, I have a pretty good idea of the kind of job that I can have without a degree. Even the employment agencies were telling me to go back to school.

However, I had been extremely interested in playing the flute, and I was not sure how helpful school would be (even if it were possible to change my major).

At this point, music is a hobby for me. I do not think music could ever be my whole future, and I doubt that it ever could have been. At any rate, music is no longer an alternative to school.

Nevertheless, I have had many doubts about school, apart from the nonacademic alternatives. One of my feelings was that psychology (partly because it is a young science, and partly because it is an intrinsically difficult one) was not very practical—that it did not deal with "basic" problems. I also found that most of my colleagues were more science-minded than I; but social relations seemed too imprecise a field.

Recently, though, I have taken a somewhat broader view, and I have begun to think that I can find my niche somewhere in psychology. At the same time, I do not consider the decision to be irrevocable in terms of my future as a whole.

I feel confident that, if I return to school next fall, I will be able to complete my work satisfactorily. I am in much less of a fog now than at any time while at Harvard, yet I do not have an overdriven quality that I had a year ago. I think I will do better and enjoy my work more. If, on the other hand, I am overly optimistic, it might be possible to have my course load reduced in the spring semester, as I have only six full courses to complete my degree requirements.

In any case, I plan to review psychology this summer. I need to prepare for the general examinations, and I want to form a better idea about the kind of graduate work I may wish to do.

In the days preceding the pilgrimage, his anxieties were increasingly visible and disheartening. On the morning he left, he was wan and silent, yet apparently determined to prove that he could handle things.

At midday he telephoned me from Cambridge. He said that along the way he had realized that he wasn't ready to go back. I urged him to keep his scheduled appointments in order to preserve his future options; he did so, and later seemed relieved that he had at least done that much. His interviews appeared to have been friendly and sympathetic. At no point, it must be said, did anyone at Harvard ever treat him as if he were a hopeless case and destroy his dreams of achieving a degree. But he obtained no clear assurance of readmission.

The crack-up came over Memorial Day weekend, which we spent together in Westport. Immediately on arrival, it was evident that Michael was almost wholly irrational again. He was playing his flute grimly and obsessively. In the middle of one night we found him in the driveway performing on it while standing on top of our car. During the day he walked around the neighborhood, suddenly pausing to aim his music at startled passers-by and dogs. Before making a call to Dr. First, he carefully arranged musical instruments in various places around the room, as if he were rehearsing to give First a telephonic concert.

Soon after returning to the city, he saw Dr. First. We talked with Dr. Sixth, and it was agreed that Michael required hospitalization again.

A few moments after our arrival at Fairhope, a young woman internist led Michael into a vacant room. I heard her begin the familiar interrogation and I could not refrain from intervening. I explained that his history was painfully well known to the hospital and implored her not to subject him to what appeared to be her own on-the-job training exercise. At that juncture Michael was himself hardly disposed to provide any lucid answers to a repetitious cross-examination.

Soon after Michael's hospitalization Betty called me. She seemed quite troubled and said there was something she urgently wanted to talk to me about that might have some bearing on Michael's breakdown. When we met, she explained that she and Michael had finally had intercourse a few days before his breakdown. She thought that the responsibility associated with this involvement might have partially provoked his dissarray. She is a shy person with great personal dignity and this confessional was recited with obvious difficulty. Naturally I did not press her for details, but she volunteered to talk with Dr. Sixth if he wanted to ask her about the relationship.

To my astonishment, Dr. Sixth was initially not interested in seeing her. He did not explain why he considered her role irrelevant, but by now we were accustomed to such enigmatic psychiatric rebuffs. When I pressed him, however, he did agree to talk with her. Most of the thirty-minute conversation, she told me later, focused on her own psychiatric history and her sexual relations with Michael.

Was the conjuncture of his night with Betty and the long weeks of tension over Harvard the cause of the collapse? No one

volunteered an answer. But now, after about nine months of renewed treatment by Dr. First, in consultation with Dr. Sixth,
Michael seemed to be back where he had been on that night in
1965 when the police apprehended him. And again we faced the
question—since Fairhope was only a temporary refuge—of
where he would go from there.

Michael was clearly afflicted once more by the paranoia that
shadowed his last days in the East Village. In many respects his
relapse was especially frightening because it could not be traced
to LSD or marijuana, as in 1965. He was again convinced that
he was being watched (by FBI agents and others) from the roof-
tops of other buildings. He told Dr. First that he again suspected Nancy of being an FBI emissary; during her visits he
nervously called her attention to the closed-circuit installations
in the patients' rooms. Of course, he was being watched, but not
by the FBI; he was under "suicide watch" with day and night
attendants.

We now centered our hopes on Dr. Sixth, who, in effect,
moved from his role as consultant to Dr. First into direct
charge. Although Dr. First continued to visit Michael, it was Dr.
Sixth with whom we usually conferred alone about new hospital
alternatives.

Dr. Sixth advanced the view that Michael needed more dis-
cipline and direction in treatment. He also said he had achieved
some success with schizophrenic patients through the use of insulin-shock therapy.

Up until this point the word *schizophrenia* had rarely been
applied to Michael in our presence by the long succession of
therapists we had encountered, but now Dr. Sixth employed it
freely. In a way it seemed a relief to have a diagnosis offered.
Schizophrenia was not considered incurable. Unfortunately, as
we were to discover later, neither is it very precisely definable
—sometimes it appears to be a code word expressing psychiatric
bewilderment over the failure of usual methods.

Although we knew little about the insulin method, we were
intrigued by Dr. Sixth's suggestion. By now Michael had under-
gone many varieties of conventional psychiatric treatment; despite all the intervals when he had seemed to be getting somewhere, there had been nothing that could be identified as

lasting improvement. With each reversal his own apprehensions
must have grimly multiplied, perhaps in part because of his own
readings in psychology and the specter of irremediable
"madness"—a word he used often—that he detected in those
pages.

Dr. First, now a somewhat occasional participant in the discussions, said he knew nothing about insulin therapy and expressed skepticism about it. But Dr. Sixth pressed the contention
that this technique, even when minimally effective, advanced
schizophrenic patients to a point at which conventional therapy
could be more effective.

In introducing the idea Dr. Sixth said he had especially high
regard for an insulin-oriented hospital in Switzerland. Despite
Dr. First's coolness to the suggestion, we responded favorably
and urged Dr. Sixth to try to arrange for Michael's acceptance
there. The only alternatives were conventional institutions similar to those in which Michael had already spent so much fruit-
less time.

After a few weeks, Dr. Sixth told us that the Swiss project
was not feasible; the doctor there in whom he had special confidence had ceased to be active. We then recalled that a state-run
hospital—Brightlawn—had a special insulin-therapy unit. In
1965, we both remembered, the resident at Fairhope had affirma-
tively mentioned the same institution. We had perhaps naïvely
recoiled from the notion of subjecting Michael to this kind of
shock program and, when we found that he could gain admission to the more celebrated halls of Statewide, we had banished
any thoughts of Brightlawn.

Now we were older, and the Statewide experience had deepened our distrust of prestigious orthodoxy and enhanced our re-
ceptivity to fresh approaches. (In fact, of course, the insulin
method was not new; but it was to people like us to whom psychiatry meant Freud and his diverse disciples.) And our reservations about the choice were largely dissolved by our meeting
with the man who presided over the Brightlawn unit and who
was to become Dr. Seventh.

We talked with Dr. Seventh in his midtown office. He told
us that many, but not all, of the patients on his ward received
insulin therapy. But he emphasized that family involvement in

the therapeutic process, including group sessions and active participation through a parent organization in the activities of the hospital, was essential. He would not consider admitting Michael unless we were prepared to devote time and concentration to the effort. He also stressed that there would be no privileges for Michael because of my newspaper position.

Our response was affirmative and eager. His forthright, pragmatic, innovative spirit seemed far removed from the often remote ambiguity we had found among other therapists. He was a warm, appealing man who communicated a sense of strength and dedication as well as a certain mirthful disdain for protocol and jargon alike.

But Michael, still at Fairhope, still skeptical of new "magic," was hesitant and ambivalent. Through the patient grapevine he had apparently heard that Brightlawn was a "tough" institution. Dr. Seventh visited him and talked bluntly and directly about the demands that his patients had to countenance, but he put the program in terms of a challenge. Rather adroitly, we thought, he also brought with him an attractive nurse, as if to counter the underground rumors that life at Brightlawn lacked a brighter side.

Dr. Sixth was increasingly enthusiastic about the move and we assumed that Dr. First, however grudgingly, was prepared to cooperate in persuading Michael to accept the transfer. But it was not quite that simple, as I discovered when I went to see Michael at Fairhope to confirm the completion of the arrangements.

On arrival I found him lying in bed with Dr. First seated beside him, the doctor's arm extended behind Michael's head. As I began to explain the details of the transfer, Michael began to protest, and Dr. First almost immediately identified himself with the objection. "I thought Dr. Sixth was making arrangements for him to go to Switzerland," he said with some asperity.

Perhaps that is what he still really thought. Although Dr. First and Dr. Sixth were presumably in communication, it was no longer quite clear when they were actually communing or sulking in their relationship with each other.

But whatever his innocence of the facts, Dr. First's response re-created the adversary mood that had recurred so often when he served in effect as Michael's attorney.

I tried, probably not very successfully, to conceal my fury at his remark. Surely he must have realized that he was rendering a difficult encounter even more painful. Moreover, he had no alternatives to present. He knew that hospitalization was essential. He knew that Fairhope would retain Michael for only a brief period.

Remembering the admonitions of both Drs. Sixth and Seventh, I simulated firmness, and once again I had the dreary sense that Michael was viewing me as his enemy while Dr. First assumed the role of sympathetic counsel and, I suppose it must be added, good father. There is probably no other satisfactory way of explaining the intensity of the conflict. When Michael needed help, it was Dr. First to whom he almost invariably sought to turn. When it became apparent that Brightlawn was designated as the next stop in his melancholy journey, it was Dr. First who seemed to be standing at his side resisting our machinations and those of other doctors to whom Dr. First was formally—but never finally—abdicating.

I wish I knew how this combat could have been conciliated. Such knowledge might assist others caught in the same trap— not others like Dr. First or myself, but like Michael. For he was the continuing victim of this interminable clash.

Dr. First's devotion to Michael was intense, far beyond any requirements of professional duty. On one occasion, in a conference with Dr. Fifth and myself at which we were discussing the wisdom of Michael's continuing to remain at home, he said he wished he could arrange for Michael to move into his home. (He was married and had one very young child.) The suggestion was no doubt a genuine expression of affection and concern. But it would, I assume, be difficult for any parent to be told that his son would find life more congenial living in the home of his psychiatrist rather than with his parents.

Yet I was continually troubled by Dr. First's intimation that my lack of faith in him and my hostility to him were damaging to Michael. As noted earlier, he had rejected Nancy's attempt at mediation. And so there would be attempts to mollify him that usually ended in fiasco. A few days before this final meeting at Fairhope, I had seen him there on a visit to Michael. In a rather self-conscious attempt to display my appreciation for his presence during another time of stress, I grasped his hand warmly. He remarked, "My, what a strong grip you have." I do not know whether the comment was diagnostic or descriptive. I was speechless.

Now, in that late afternoon when Michael was looking at me as if I were the hanging judge pronouncing his jail sentence while Dr. First vainly sought to protect him, I did not know whether I would weep or explode. (Much later, in family discussions with Dr. Seventh at which Michael intimated a desire to return to Dr. First, Dr. Seventh characterized the relationship between Dr. First and Michael as "unhealthy." Curiously, Michael did not dissent or prolong the argument. Dr. Seventh was saying aloud what I had been thinking for a long time and guiltily suppressing lest it be deemed a reflection of my own envy of Michael's confidence in his adopted father.)

I left Michael without yielding to his pleas for reprieve from Brightlawn. His farewell to Dr. First was genial and intimate. His cryptic good-by to me needed no annotation.

At home, I told Nancy of the muted contretemps. Yet I felt a need for corroboration and proposed that we call Dr. First. I spoke with him first; I made clear my dismay and bitterness over the negative role he had played. I told him that I did not see how he could remain in the case any longer without obstructing the new effort that Dr. Seventh was about to initiate at Brightlawn. He did not contest my account of what had occurred, nor did he do so when Nancy took the phone. It was she who then said, even more emphatically than I, that he was no longer to consider himself Michael's doctor.

(In a volume, *Up from Depression*, that we read after Michael's death, Dr. Leonard Cammer argues that it is vital to successful therapy that there be an easy relationship between parents and the doctor they have chosen for their child. 'If you believe that more could be done for your relative's depression or that another therapist's treatment program might be better, take your ideas directly to the doctor," he wrote. But the recommendation is hardly helpful when the child has in effect selected his psychiatrist and when the psychiatrist insists that he be allowed to proceed without meeting the parents.)

Dr. First was apparently stunned by Nancy's edict and the united front it signified. It was always my sense that he regarded her as his ultimate ally in the duel to which he and I intermittently reverted. The next morning he called her at her office. She said, "Hello, Dr. First, how are you?" He replied, "I'm all shook up."

He said he wanted to make certain that she had really meant to say that he was out of the case. She reiterated the decision. We did not hear from Dr. First again before or after Michael's death.

XI

Alone Again

BRIGHTLAWN had the dreary, prisonlike exterior of most large state institutions. Dr. Seventh had agreed to drive Michael out, and I went along; the shock of its surface was more acute with Michael at my side. As we approached it, I could hardly bear to look at him; what he saw must have confirmed the worst things he had heard from the grapevine in the plush setting of Fairhope. While there were large grounds and a park across the street, this forbidding series of structures must have seemed an especially long and depressing distance from the country-club landscape at Pleasant View, his first experience with hospitalization three years earlier.

Michael made it clear on arrival that he was not ready for insulin-shock therapy, and Dr. Seventh did not press him. There were positive signs in the apparent rapport that Dr. Seventh established with him. As Michael's psychotic manifestations diminished, he seemed to begin to envisage himself as something of a deputy to the doctor.

In August of that summer Holly was married to David Karpf. The joy of the day was dimmed by Michael's absence, but it was Dr. Seventh's judgment, in which we concurred, that it would be unwise for him to attend. The event would have only accentuated for Michael the poignancy of his own predicament; to return to Brightlawn after such festivity might have been unbearable. In any case, we were relieved that he did not seem disposed to argue the point after what Dr. Seventh felt was a somewhat *pro forma* appeal to be liberated for that day.

On the weekend of the wedding, in a somewhat lame effort to minimize the special loneliness he must have endured at that moment, I wrote him:

I hope you know how much Mother, Holly, and I are thinking of you on this weekend and how much we wish that you were with us. I know that you tried to get permission to attend the wedding and, of course, we were disappointed that you didn't succeed.

The only solace we have is the very real feeling of confidence we have acquired about Brightlawn, confirmed by what we have heard from many parents at our meetings there, and our own feeling about the human qualities of Dr. Seventh. I can only add that we will do all we can to cooperate and hasten the day when you will be well and free, and when the spirit and fortitude you have shown in this long trial will be rewarded. And so this is just to say again how much we miss you and how we look forward to the time when there will be a comparable weekend for you. . . .

One could never be sure whether such words were a comfort or an irritant, especially at a time when Michael's relationship with Betty was slowly crumbling. A few months earlier, it had seemed possible to visualize them on a wedding day; after Michael entered Brightlawn, Betty became a diligent visitor, and they also corresponded frequently. Her home was almost at the opposite end of the city, and the trips must have been long and tedious and particularly shattering when Michael used their meetings to hint at liaisons with female patients. Some of his letters to her were also tantalizing. Thus, on September 9, he wrote her from Westport, where he was visiting us on a weekend pass:

How are you? Why can't you visit a bit sooner? Etc.? Am in shitty mood; in Westport. I get weekend passes now. . . . Last weekend I brought a nice girl up here (with another couple)—hope you're jealous. Why not visit sooner?

Love Mike

But there would also be small, elusive love-rhymes:

Poem to Betty
Why so glum my teedle-dum?
Why so sad my crazy pad?
Why so little, next to me?
Why not take a sip and see?

In October Betty finally decided she could not endure the strain and ambiguity any longer. She conscientiously called us to tell us that she had written a farewell letter to Michael. We asked her to come over and talk about it before mailing it, but she said she could not waver any longer. She did, however, bring us a typed copy of the letter. It read:

Dear Michael,

I am writing this letter to you instead of telling you because I know what I have to say will depress you and I think it would be better if you were to receive it at the hospital. To put it bluntly, I feel it is better if we don't see each other anymore. I don't want to lie to you and say it is only because of my anxiety every time I see you that has brought about this decision, because it is a lot more than that.

I feel a relationship has got to be nearly total communication between two people, and we no longer have that. I am unable to tell you what I think about anything but the most superficial matters, because as soon as I disagree with you you tell me to "shut my fucking mouth, you don't know anything about it" or go off and play your flute. This isn't communication and doesn't do either of us any good. I'm not a three-year-old who is satisfied with side-by-side play, I have to interact with somebody.

Your attempts to make me jealous are another thing I can't cope with. On the one hand you tell me about all the girls you meet at the hospital and outside and the next minute you want to make love to me. The two things just don't go together. Not telling me about them if you were thinking about them would be dishonest and wouldn't work either. What bothers me is that you are not ready to relate to one woman. You apologize and tell me they don't mean anything to you and you are just reliving your adolescence. If that's what you want to do—O.K. but don't expect me to relive mine. I'm twenty-four and want a relationship with a man who is mature enough to handle a real involvement with another human being. When I do go out with other men, you constantly question me and try to make me feel guilty. Michael, I am sorry you are sick, I am sorry you are in the hospital, but it is unfair to ask me to build a shell around myself until you get better. I've got my own life to lead and my first loyalty is to myself.

I know you are going to think this is unfair and that I've deserted you. But maybe in your own way you deserted me. What we had was very good, and I loved you. But it is useless not to face reality. You're a fine human being and you've got an awful lot to give somebody. I hope someday you'll be able to.

Best of luck.

Betty

Saddened as we were by these farewell words, we could not quarrel with what she had done or implore her to retract; we were grateful for the sensitivity she had shown. We were often to wonder thereafter whether Dr. First's warnings to Michael about his involvement with Betty had helped to destroy whatever chance there may have been for preservation of this fragile but unmistakably genuine and initially promising union.

This is not to say that we could simplistically attribute the breakup to Dr. First's intrusion; Betty had herself speculated that their climactic night together may have been in some measure responsible for Michael's crack-up. Her portrait of his reluctance to "relate to one woman" was undoubtedly perceptive. But to what extent were Dr. First's admonitions a factor in promoting rather than diminishing Michael's incapacity to "relate"?

Now the questions will never be satisfactorily answered. We did not raise them when it might have mattered.

XII

Episode at a Window

As THE Brightlawn period began, Dr. Seventh quickly confirmed our belief that he had no spiritual bonds with nearly all
the therapists we had known.

He was a dominant, paternal, inexhaustible, beguiling figure,
the inspiration for staff, patients, and parents alike. His undis-
guised vanity was mercifully tempered by humor and—at certain doleful moments—humility. He was implausibly ubiqui-
tous. He ran the large Sunday sessions of family and patients,
which had the mingled quality of revival meetings, pep rallies,
and seminars.

There were certain messages that he steadfastly tried to communicate at these general conclaves and in the smaller group-
therapy gatherings over which he presided. One was that there
could be no tolerance for shame among parents whose children
were in his care. He understood that society frequently dealt
coldly and harshly with former inmates when they sought employment or even acceptance, but it was our obligation to fight
the stigma by frank avowals. We were not to pretend that our
children were skiing in Switzerland when they were patients at
Brightlawn. One technique for affirming our involvement was
the sale of raffle tickets for hospital bazaars—there was to be no
dissembling about the nature of the institution benefiting from
the commerce.

Dr. Seventh did not believe in individual, patient-to-doctor
therapy; he thought that kind of treatment kept schizophrenic
patients dependent without solving their problems. He relied instead on a combination of insulin shock, electric shock, or other
drug treatment, and family therapy. He thought patients must
be brought to accept responsibility for making their own adjustment back into the world, even by use of quite drastic methods.

But the most fundamental distinction in Dr. Seventh's approach emerged quickly during the family therapy conferences. They often produced recrimination and rancor from the patients, and sometimes from the parents, but, after permitting the storm to rage for a while, Dr. Seventh invariably reverted to this challenge to the patients: "All right, this is how you feel about the past. The question is, what do you do now? Do you want to get well? It will do you no good to keep talking about what happened before. What happens now?"

There were two kinds of family therapy programs. One involved a group of three, four, and five families (patient and parents, or patient plus spouse) meeting with a therapist. The other brought together a large number of family groups, as many as fifteen or twenty. In the larger conclaves the technique was to have one family act as a model and focus of discussion for each session, with the therapist encouraging and stimulating relatively frank and full disclosure by the family, and explicit criticism and comment from the rest of the people. We observed only one or two such sessions and have no way of appraising their effectiveness. We did come away with the feeling that such open, full talk about these problems was helpful for the parents who were able to exchange with others feelings too long repressed and festering. But we cannot tell whether it was, in the long run, of much value for the patients.

Given a choice of which kind of "multiple-family therapy" we wanted—the big group or the small—we chose the latter. We were in a group of five families: the M's and their daughter; the B's and their son; the L's and their daughter; and the J's and their son. M.M. was a girl of about seventeen or eighteen who was bright, talented, very disturbed, and volatile; S.B. was a boy of about nineteen or twenty who was not catatonic, but seemed at times to verge on it, although he could also be lucid and fluent; the L. girl was about twenty-seven, but was mentally retarded as well as mentally ill so that she acted like the youngest of the group and was incapable of communicating on anything beyond an infantile level; H.J. was a boy of about twenty-five who had sunk into deterioration that was both physical and mental—he hardly ever said anything at all and when he did he was almost incomprehensible. The group therapist was Dr. Seventh. There was usually a nurse or other staff person present. Dr. Seventh taped the sessions, which lasted about an hour and a half. They were held every other Sunday after the obligatory parent-patient general meeting. Since H.J. and the L. girl were really incapable of participating, the three patients who were in any sense active participants in the group were Mike, M.M., and S.B. Most of the parents, including the parents of the nonparticipant patients, were fairly active.

We were apprehensive about these sessions before they began. We anticipated searing confrontations, embarrassment, upheavals. It did not work out that way. Partly perhaps because the M and B families tended to be the focus of the meetings, we were spared. We also suspect Dr. Seventh was easier on us than on the others because I was a journalist. It might have been much better for Michael if this had not happened, hard as it might have been for us. He saw Dr. Seventh probing quite sharply with the M and the B families, but treading softly with the Wechslers. Perhaps Dr. Seventh had good reason for this leniency; perhaps pressure would not have been helpful. But in time Michael seemed to feel that Dr. Seventh was more *our* doctor than his. This also tended to reinforce some of the problems which arose from Michael's unfortunate choice of two rather strong-minded, articulate parents.

During the first few multiple-family gatherings Mike was rather active and said some things that were revealing to us. Thus at one session he said that he might have been interested in journalism but felt his father would resent it. We had always thought that we were leaning over backward to avoid pressuring Mike in any career direction. Much as I would have been delighted if he cared about entering my profession, it seemed important not to be exhorting him to do so.

After his death, we found a psychology paper written early in his Harvard years dealing with "the genesis of intellectual motivation." In it there appeared this passage:

Our main thesis will be that people with high anxiety about competition will tend to choose intellectual motives other than his father's [*sic*]. Since we have assumed that the reason for this type of identification is related to gaining the mother's affection, then it is to some degree aggressive in nature. Thus, insofar as there is anxiety about aggression toward the father, identification which implies aggression will be avoided. We might have to modify our theory by substituting competition with a male, or older male. We are really trying to measure a childhood conflict, and we are hoping that it is still latent in some way.

Though there is no literature specifically relevant, there is literature supporting the idea of (male) identification with the father being the normal course. Psychoanalysts do not tend to support the idea presented here concerning the avoidance of identification that is associated with aggression; but I am not sure that this concept is refuted by them. When the father is felt as threatening, he is identified with, but in just what way is unclear. I have as yet seen no examples where the increase of identification favors competition with the felt aggressor; sometimes mention is made of a strict introjection of the father's "superego."

There is also the possibility of male identification with a female relative, which probably would not bear on our theory; we would have to find out to what extent this actually exists.

Much more might have happened at Brightlawn, with perhaps real therapeutic value, if these sessions had been held more systematically. Certainly the multiple-family technique seemed generally constructive for Michael as well as for us. Unfortunately, the sessions occurred only every two weeks; not infrequently they were canceled.

Our group also had the distinction but perhaps also the misfortune of being the subject of an experiment in filming multiple-family therapy. As a result much time and attention were devoted to getting the sessions on film, and less to any therapeutic exploration. It was in that interval that we began to feel a new uneasiness. Dr. Seventh's insight and devotion were plain, but we also began to see that much of his boundless energy was invested in research projects or experiments such as the filming—sometimes at the expense of sustained therapy.

It took Michael several weeks to agree to the insulin treatments. This was not uncommon and surely understandable, Dr. Seventh explained. After they began, he appeared less fearful of them and even expressed a certain pleasure about the sodium amytal ("truth serum") sometimes given afterward.

Did the insulin device help him even temporarily? Again, there is no precise measurement. We don't remember exactly

how many insulin treatments Mike had before he left Brightlawn. It was fewer than Dr. Seventh had initially recommended, and we will never know whether more would have
helped. While Dr. Seventh believed in insulin treatment plus
family therapy (but not individual therapy), Dr. Sixth had origi-
nally suggested insulin not as an independent therapeutic factor
but as a prerequisite to further individual therapy. Thus these
two doctors were in basic disagreement about the purpose of the
insulin usage—a dispute that must have been evident to Michael.

When Michael arrived at Brightlawn he had many manifestations that evoked the description "psychotic." Soon after reaching there he was announcing that he wanted to leave at once
and get back to Harvard, oblivious to the fact that he had not
been readmitted. Yet gradually there was unmistakable progress, as if the cloud were lifting again. Michael seemed to become a member of the community that Dr. Seventh was trying
to create. He helped with patients who were most outwardly
disturbed, contributed poems to the mimeographed newspaper
published by the patients, and socialized with patients and
pretty occupational therapy assistants. He began receiving
weekend passes and was permitted to attend the wedding of
Nancy's brother. Unfortunately, almost as soon as he arrived, a
relative of the bride asked him, "And what do you do?" Such
questions were always a terrible reminder of the second-class
citizenship occupied by mental patients.

There were also reminders that his comparatively quiescent
exterior did not signify any final triumph. During a number of
our visits he was aloof and combative and would pointedly find
reasons for leaving us alone while he roamed around. In mid-
November there was a pre-Thanksgiving theatrical program produced and performed by the patients. Although there had been
earlier announcements that Michael would play the flute in one
episode, he told us when we arrived that he had decided not to
participate.

We never really knew whether such abstentions indicated
anxieties far more profound than any conventional stage fright
or whether they were, in part, a rebellion against the notion of
being placed on exhibition.

But just as he seemed to be wholly "cured" of his psychotic symptoms and to have acquired a new surface of calm, his restlessness reasserted itself. He was granted a long weekend of freedom for Thanksgiving. Yet, as these periods of authorized liberty multiplied, his reluctance to go back when the time out was over increased.

After about three months at Brightlawn, he receded into depression, not as deep or dramatic as when he was at Statewide, but persistent and stubborn and unrelieved either by continued insulin treatment or by family therapy. It was around that time that Betty had broken off with him. Perhaps it was triggered by that rebuff, but perhaps it was a resistance to, almost a fear of, "getting better" and being obliged to confront new challenges without any interior confidence. Dr. Seventh thought Michael could not bring himself to cut off his reliance on us and that we contributed to this by overprotecting him and refusing to force him to be independent.

Dr. Seventh insisted that Michael at least receive the full schedule of insulin dosages before any discussion of release took place. Michael argued with rising vehemence that whatever had been accomplished was being undermined by keeping him there. His impatience and irritation mounted. At times he would attribute this to the fact that "my girl friend left me." But more and more he would exclaim reproachfully to Dr. Seventh, "If only you'd let me out when I felt better. It's this hospital that's depressing me."

There seemed some surface validity in the complaint. It was in many ways a bleak place; as in so many state institutions, there must always be the paradox that a patient who begins to feel well becomes suddenly more conscious of the drabness of the setting and the seemingly hopeless sickness of those around him who have experienced no comparable symptoms of rejuvenation. Yet many of the patients seemed to be progressing. At what point is recovery obstructed by the fact that the inmate's new rationality enables him more clearly to discern his predicament? He feels too well to be confined, yet is judged not really well enough to be freed.

Then a sudden tragedy hit the ward: the suicide of Kenneth. It may be that this disaster both deepened Michael's distrust of the treatment and reduced his desire for liberation. Michael and Kenneth were both "Harvard men"; a visitor would also have seen them as more "normal" than many other inmates. They were generally fastidious about their appearance and usually silent in the large, sometimes combative Sunday sessions. We had come to know Kenneth's mother, a gracious, attractive woman who served as a volunteer worker at the hospital. She was divorced from her husband and had another son who had fled to Canada as a draft resister. But she always seemed a model of composure and restraint, utterly free of self-pity.

There was no indication that Michael and Kenneth had established any close friendship. Perhaps their Harvard histories had made each unduly self-conscious in the presence of the other, or perhaps they were still too withdrawn to welcome what would have seemed a logical association.

Then, while at home on a pass, Kenneth plunged out of a window of his mother's home and died instantly.

It seemed clear when we broached the subject that Michael did not want to talk about it and, as in so many other critical interludes, we abandoned the discussion hastily. Now one wonders whether he might have viewed our reticence as an evasion or further lack of comprehension of his own torment.

Kenneth's mother stoically reappeared at the hospital and resumed her work there without any extended interruption. Dr. Seventh, addressing the patients, voiced appropriate sentiments of grief but insisted in somewhat melodramatic fashion that Kenneth was a "casualty" in the war against mental illness, and the rest of us could now only resolve to redouble our efforts, whether as parents or patients. Michael listened stolidly, as did most of the others. One could not know how many were thinking, "There but for the grace of God. . . ."

For many weeks before that disaster, Michael had been avowing his loss of faith in any miracle at Brightlawn and his resentment over his failure to win earlier release. He did not use Kenneth's death as the occasion for any new or strident demands for freedom; possibly he assumed that his message needed no elaboration.

Yet each of his now regular weekends at home seemed to involve greater tension as the moment approached for the return trip. (The patients were required to sign in at 8:00 P.M. on Sunday evening.)

When he came home there was little for him to do. Betty would not see him, although he called her a number of times. Occasionally Holly and her husband came to town from their Long Island home. Once in a while Michael arranged for some activity with another patient who was on pass; on rare occasions he saw an old friend.

Finally, on a Sunday afternoon in late February, Michael began to express more emphatically than before an unwillingness to go back. We talked quietly for a while, reviewing all the old arguments about the unwisdom, as well as the illegality, of defiance. Then, as we had on several previous Sundays, we stopped the debate, as if by mutual agreement, or exhaustion, and proceeded as if we were adhering to schedule. When we had finished dinner, Nancy headed for the garage to get the car. Michael went to his room, presumably to pack his suitcase; he indicated no plan for last-ditch resistance as Nancy left.

But several moments passed and he failed to emerge. Apprehensively, I opened his door and walked into his room. He was sitting on the windowsill of our ninth-floor apartment, and though it was a cold, rainy winter night, the window was wide open. I quietly reminded him that it was time to leave. He said he would be ready in a few minutes. With new foreboding, I left him alone, presumably while he packed his bag. But when he did not reappear quickly, I went back. He had not moved from the window.

This, I suppose, was the way I imagined (wrongly) that it had been on that first day so long ago when he had telphoned me and announced his desperate need for immediate psychiatric help. But this time he was there, nine floors above ground, the window open, and fifteen feet separating us.

In as controlled a voice as I could achieve, I asked him to close the window and talk things over. After a brief hesitation, he left the precarious site and walked into the room. Then I made a mistake. I said, "Mike, you know you have to go back, please stop threatening me." The words seemed to incite some deep rage or desperation.

Suddenly he was running across the room and toward the

window. His legs dangled from the ledge and then I was there with my arms around his neck dragging him back. I believe he had started to slide downward (he was later to say I exaggerated how far he had gone). In any case, I pulled him frantically and we both landed on the floor, my arms still clutching him, and he was looking at me, crying: "Dad, why didn't you let me go?"

Never before nor thereafter had we held each other so warmly and agonizingly as we did in that moment. And then he seemed to find a great calm. We got up together and went back into the living room. I suggested that we both needed a drink and he responded eagerly to the proposal.

We talked easily, in friendly, quiet tones, as if that crisis had given us a new intimacy. We agreed that the episode had created the immediate, serious procedural problem that he would be placed in the "security" ward when he got back to Brightlawn (his return was no longer in dispute). We agreed that Dr. Seventh would have to be told what had happened, but that he might be persuaded to believe that the danger point was passed. We also agreed that the first step was to go downstairs together before Nancy began to worry about our delay.

She was seated in the car, just a few feet from the place where Michael would have fallen. When we reached her, I said that we had all better go back to the apartment and I explained on the way up what had occurred. The three of us talked a while longer before I called Dr. Sixth, who recommended that I report what had happened to Dr. Seventh at once. In that period of reprieve and relief, we seemed like three coconspirators joined to protect Michael from excessive punishment.

Dr. Seventh came over quickly. He called the hospital and cleared Michael's name for late arrival.

Many weeks later, after Michael had left Brightlawn and returned to live at home with us, Dr. Seventh delivered another pronouncement. Michael was expressing renewed despair about his chances for real recovery and Dr. Seventh was assuring him that he no longer suffered from any ailment except his own lack of resolve to live. He told him he had three clear choices—to function in the real world, to be a permanent hospital patient, or to destroy himself.

"It's up to you, Mike," he said, "but if you decide you don't want to live, for God's sake, don't jump out the window. You might fail and end up a cripple, and then you'd be worse. Just take pills and do a good job."

I wanted to say that this seemed a poor statement of the issues. After all, to tell Michael that he was "cured"—when he plainly did not feel that way—was almost a form of simple-minded Couéism; it perhaps also strengthened his belief that Dr. Seventh was our doctor, not his. But I suppose that by then I accepted such an utterance as an enlightened form of "shock treatment": indeed, Dr. Seventh may have succeeded in other cases by resort to such direct challenge. Perhaps he felt that the time had come to gamble on this approach. I didn't say anything; neither did Nancy. Did Michael construe our silence as an ultimate failure of comprehension, and even a bland reconciliation to Dr. Seventh's statement of the alternatives?

XIII

The Last Love Story

THE IMMEDIATE RESULT of the window crisis was that Michael was required to accept a sixty-day, unconditional commitment period. Dr. Seventh quite reasonably contended that he had, to some degree, covered up for Michael by not putting the full details on record and thereby sparing him an extended term in dreaded maximum security.

But as the end of the sixty days neared, Michael resumed his fight for release. Dr. Seventh advanced the compromise that Michael be transferred to Grace Hill—a small, rather luxurious, and very expensive private enclave in the city—as a halfway house toward total liberation. Dr. Seventh suggested that Michael use the transition at Grace Hill to begin the search for employment that would justify final discharge. Meanwhile, Dr. Seventh would serve as his private therapist.

Shortly before the transfer, the four of us had a consultation at Dr. Seventh's office in Brightlawn. The doctor insisted that Michael's stay at Grace Hill be devoted to curing what he considered Michael's dependence on us—the "cotton-batting" of protection at home. He suggested that we avoid seeing Michael at all for a month. The suggestion seemed to frighten Michael, and we did not accept it.

Dr. Seventh then came up with another formula. He was planning a film explaining certain techniques of "system" analysis that he was promoting. He needed someone to transform sketches he had drafted into large charts, and he was convinced Michael could handle the job. If he did so satisfactorily, there would be a place for him in the further development of the project. Under the plan, Dr. Seventh would pay Michael a regular salary, for which we would reimburse him without Michael's knowledge.

Nancy recalls Michael's interview with the admitting doctor at Grace Hill, in which Michael agreed that the objective of the stay there was articulated as "last hospital and out."

But time had rendered it harder for Michael to go out into the world looking for work. The inevitable problem was how to explain himself: Where was he supposed to have been during the past four years? He felt unequal to brazening out any plausible evasions. He pursued one or two leads, but nothing came of them. After a couple of weeks he made no progress. So Dr. Seventh's make-work program seemed the best alternative.

But the plan didn't work. Michael resisted it, claiming that he couldn't understand what he was supposed to do (although it was the sort of work he could have done very easily in an earlier time). His depression continued and he showed increasing signs of deserting Dr. Seventh. Finally the doctor decided that modified electric-shock therapy should be used to combat the depression. A specialist at the hospital gave Mike a series of about six shock treatments, after which the melancholy did indeed seem to recede.

Meanwhile, I had been talking to Moe Foner, a good friend who is a leading figure in the Hospital Workers Union and who knew the management at Grace Hill. Through his efforts Michael was given a chance to work in the occupational therapy room as a kind of general assistant to the director of the OT program. While Michael was unenthusiastic about this work, he found it tolerable. He became friendly with other ex-patients who worked in a similar capacity, and he acquired a feeling of responsibility for the OT shop and for the patients who came there. Dr. Seventh told Mike that he would agree to discharge him from the hospital after he had worked at this job for a limited time.

The question then arose of where Mike would live after the release and what kind of follow-up therapy would take place. Dr. Seventh told Mike that he had the option of continuing with him or finding a new therapist, and he also said that he would continue as family therapist if we wanted him to do so. Dr. Seventh also recommended that Michael not live at home, in line with his theory that such patients would not really get better while they were dependent on their families. The patient should be on his own, "responsible for himself," even if family subsidy was needed. But we could not accept the idea that Michael, after over a year in hospitals, with no base, no circle of friends, and so long out of touch with the world, should be left to go it alone so abruptly. We feared a renewed depression and possible involvement with drugs. Michael came home and continued to go to work at the hospital every day.

There followed a few months somewhat similar to earlier periods. Michael was functioning to some extent and making some effort to establish some sort of social life, but it was a bleak time. He would go to publicly advertised parties for "singles" but come home discouraged and disconsolate. He had lost contact with society for so long that it was hard for him to find any common ground with people he found at such places.

All those cumulative months of illness and hospitalization meant that he was, often for months, either unaware or only dimly aware of what was going on in the world. Consequently, in periods of relative remission it was hard to catch up, to participate in ordinary social talk involving knowledge of contemporary events. He did try sporadically to keep informed, and from time to time he had even participated, as in the New York City Peace March in the spring of 1967. But he was not part of his time, because for so much of it he was so remote from the world, grappling with private torments. While he had some dates with fellow workers and fellow ex-patients, they led nowhere.

One night, after attending a gathering advertised in the *Village Voice*, he came home and exclaimed with heartbreaking bitterness, "You don't know what it's like to be so damn lonely." How did one answer such an outcry, beyond unsatisfactory reminders of old friends whom he might try to locate, almost all of whom now had established positions in life?

Still, he continued at his OT job and maintained a record of faithful attendance. Although he protested that he found the work uninspiring, hospital officials were gratified by his diligence and congeniality. By mid-November, Dr. Seventh was sufficiently reassured to give Michael a written testimonial required to obtain renewal of his driver's license.

Subsequent to Michael's departure from Grace Hill, the three of us had been seeing Dr. Seventh in his private office about once a month. Michael asked the doctor to renew the use of sodium amytal, and a few such sessions were held. The theory was that, under the influence of the drug, patient inhibitions would disappear, enabling the therapist to get at problems that might take an eternity of conventional psychotherapy to uncover. The doctor put these interviews on tape and Mike thought that he and the doctor would have other sessions at which the tapes would be played and discussed. That never happened and we were never told why. Michael was becoming more disenchanted with Dr. Seventh; he reiterated that he was our doctor, not his. There was talk of someone else taking over and also talk of Michael being brought into group-therapy sessions with other young people. We thought such a group might be very useful, but Dr. Seventh did not pursue the idea.

Meanwhile, growing more restive in the OT job at the hospital (clearly a dead end), Michael began to investigate computer analysis training. He took tests at a number of schools that purported to train young people for such work. It was difficult to get good information about such schools, and in the course of inquiry we heard about a job opening at a new market research organization. Michael was taken on there, and after the first few weeks of characteristic self-doubt he found that he could perform adequately.

Then, in late fall, the therapeutic structure fell apart. Dr. Seventh went away on vacation for a month, then canceled two appointments. For about eight weeks we had no word from him. Finally, he came to see us and told us that he was leaving the hospital and moving to another state. The reason he gave was that he had a commitment to finish a book. There was no explanation of the weeks of silence, of his failure to get Michael into group therapy or to make any arrangements for continued management of Michael's treatment.

We were utterly baffled, and Michael plainly felt betrayed. He decided on his own to see if Dr. Sixth would take him on as a patient. Dr. Sixth declined, saying that he was too busy devoting much of his time to a special project. But he offered to find someone else, and so, after the months of group-oriented treatment, Michael went back into the hands of a Freudian-oriented individual therapist, another 180-degree shift. Dr. Eighth was highly recommended by Dr. Sixth and had been associated with him. We hoped that somehow the effect of insulin-shock therapy and hospitalization would indeed make progress possible.

Dr. Eighth was a woman to whom Dr. Sixth frequently referred patients of his own. He told us of a case that he regarded as very similar to Michael's, a young man with long years of treatment and hospitalization, whom she had finally salvaged "in just a few months."

Once again we were reduced, or so it seemed, to a decision of faith. Dr. Sixth could not find a place for Michael in his calendar. Dr. Seventh was no longer accessible. We had irrevocably broken off relations with Dr. First. Dr. Third was in Cambridge. Michael had "fired" Dr. Second and Dr. Fourth. Dr. Fifth had left while Michael was at Statewide. And Dr. Sixth spoke convincingly of Dr. Eighth's miracle. We did not even ask to meet her until later, and then she sent word through Dr. Sixth that she thought it was inadvisable. He volunteered to continue to serve as intermediary. We went along with the arrangement. We had to assume that Dr. Sixth had fully briefed her on Michael's history—from Freud to insulin—and we felt a dull-witted relief that *someone* was again in charge. Only Holly pointedly expressed concern about the reversion to Freudian techniques.

Meanwhile, Vicky had moved into a major place in Michael's life. It is best to introduce her by printing a fragment about her that we found among Michael's papers. It must have been written in the late winter or early spring of 1969. Once again he was apparently thinking in terms of a writer's life and hoping, as he suggests in the prelude, that if he sat down at a typewriter, without outline or other planning, something important would begin to happen:

Why not start with whatever is on my mind and see what develops? Perhaps it will all lead somewhere. . . .

I still have no real idea of what will happen to me in the near future; it could be more Hell; it could be deadness, or a mixture of both. Or neither, for it could be a beautiful castle in the air—one where I think I may have, for a few moments, already have visited. As long as all does not become dead and hopeless, I have a chance for something meaningful. Still, I wonder a lot whether my only alternative to being one of the living dead is to feel only by being tortured. Tortured, it often seems, by my own hand. Or rather in the hands of those I welcome with open arms and heart. . . . Such a vulnerable little heart.

Vicky appeared in OT one day, and, though I was in my dead stage at the time (one of many such stages), I was immediately attracted to her. She struck me as pretty, though not beautiful or terribly sexy; but she was also someone, one of the few, that I could talk to fairly easily. Not that our conversations were very intense or rewarding for me; that would be difficult for someone like I was at the time: very tense, very lifeless, quite hopeless—but working, nevertheless, in the arts and craft shop ("occupational therapy") of an expensive psychiatric hospital in NYC. Working in such a place is hard if you know that you're just as screwed up as half of the patients, and, also, if you've just recently been a patient at that very same hospital. But when I was with Vicky I did not feel at a loss for words, nor did I feel that she expected me to treat her as sick and be continually kind and understanding, a model of health. In fact, by the time I met her in OT, I think she seemed considerably healthier to me than I was. She even enjoyed working with clay and paints somewhat— something I've pretty much only been able to do when I was quite flipped out. Before she left I saw her two children, and the three looked like a pretty happy group. Vicky asked if we could exchange phone numbers, and though I seem to remember being pleased at the suggestion, I forgot to give her my number after she had written down hers. She was not insulted, though; she asked for my number which I wrote apologetically. I don't think I expected to see or hear from her again; she had two kids, and I was as much afraid of responsibility as I was of people. I didn't believe I had anything to offer anybody, which was largely true. Still, I did think of her now and then. Not more than once or twice.

Then one day, a couple of months later, she called. I think I recognized her voice immediately, which doesn't mean I was a changed person from the way I was when we met at the hospital; I was still half dead, still afraid of involvement (largely the fear of not being able to return the gift of love). It was eight o'clock at night, but she wanted to come all the way to see me—a trip that can take as much as two hours by subway, and tonight was a working night for me besides. She still wanted to come, even if it were only for a few hours. Though it seemed a bit crazy to me (her having two kids and living, at least for the time, with her parents who were two hours away), I looked forward to our meeting.

I was a little tense with her at first (but I'm usually tense with anyone), but we had no trouble talking to each other, except that we probably talked more than was necessary or comfortable. At one point in the conversation she said that if we were really comfortable with each other we would not just be talking, but touching. I guess we both needed someone to touch, because a little while later I was sitting on my bed, and when she got up from her chair for a second, I asked her to sit next to me. I knew what I was really asking her, but I was not at all sure I wanted to sleep with her. But that's what we did. I was still pretty tense about being with her physically, and I could tell before we even began our intercourse that it would be over very quickly; I often come absurdly quickly, especially when I am beginning with a new girl. But that's a little easier on the ego than being impotent. . . .

With my first sexual partner, which was to begin before I began my second year of college, I was totally impotent for quite some time. But it's funny; sexual problems like those, which bother me a lot, never produced a mean or negative response to the girl involved. And they have generally worked themselves out not too badly.

But with Vicky the premature ejaculations continued for the longest time. I would also feel bad that she could not reach orgasm; but she would always be annoyed that it even worried me. And really, I know that all those problems are pretty superficial; what really matters is to have a feeling of love or at least emotional closeness during physical intimacy. All that is very trite, but it's sure important.

Besides, there is so much more to the physical side than just fucking. All the foreplay, and just the fact of being naked next to each other, holding each other, giving each other a sensual security, a tenderness mixed with passion, a togetherness that dissolves cares. Sure wish I knew more about all that; it hasn't been that way often.

I guess I called Vicky the next day, still as unsure as ever. But it had begun, and it was to continue. Two people always touching physically, but never being together (in any sense). We'd go to bed, touch, make love, and I'd go to sleep in another room. I'd have to be away from her then. There just wouldn't be enough room for both of us in one bed; I was too hemmed in, too restless. She would want me to stay

That is exactly where it ended—there was not even a period at the end of the last sentence. Perhaps, as the turbulence of their relationship mounted, Michael found it harder to continue the recital.

But a poem he wrote in the month of his death—it was dated only "May '69"—may have been a footnote:

> She called not angry, not in desperate need;
> To apologize in a twisted unapologetic scared

yet giving, though unsure. Neither of us were sure what it
really meant. Was it Heaven or Hell, sent?
I did not know what to say; I was dead, she was alive,
though scared; I tried to hide my jealousy; I tried to be
    manipulated
or manipulating
Next Morning: not stoned on Southern Comfort, and tranquil-
    izers . . .
Hurry, hurry, scurry like a rat; no need to look back
To work, where what little dream I might have now will be
jerked from my emasculated soul.
Dream? To be alive, to feel worth something, to really have
something personally and emotional to give to someone,
having no one.
Dream? Back to school and be my own fool, thinking nothing,
or thinking I can change the world.
Reality? Somewhere in the middle: no one's fool, no one's
    God.

They were a remarkably attractive couple. Seeing them together, as we did several times, an almost premonitory phrase
would keep flashing into mind: "the beautiful and the damned."
There were few outward resemblances between Vicky and
Betty. Both were what are poorly described as lovely young
women. But Betty gave a sense of strong, sturdy womanhood, almost a tintype of the "outdoor girl." Vicky was intensely, almost
theatrically feminine. And while Betty's problems, masked by
her ebullience, were real, they were incomparably less acute
than Vicky's, who had been in more than one mental hospital.
Actually, Michael's involvement with Vicky may have been
partly produced by Betty's unwillingness to see him during that
interval. When he called Betty periodically, she told him that
she had gained a great deal of weight and would be embarrassed to have him see her.

In any case, Michael's attachment for Vicky became increasingly obsessive, especially when he began to find her elusive
and tantalizing. As we try to reconstruct the events of his last
spring and last days on earth, it is hard to assess how critical
this relationship was.

For Vicky was not Michael's only disturbing preoccupation.
As in the spring of 1967, when he was wooing Betty, he was

again tormented by a sense that he was getting nowhere in life —and now he was twenty-six.

The progression of the illness had cut him off from his old friends. Each year had increased the difference between what he had failed to achieve and the normal course of life for his contemporaries. As time went on he had ceased any effort to see them. At his job there were understanding fellow workers who were friendly with Mike, but by then he could not reciprocate this attentiveness. He rebuffed their social invitations and their efforts to get him to participate in such ventures as amateur theatricals.

There are also indications, as early as March, that he feared another serious relapse or, as he bluntly stated it to Holly following a dispute over the use of the telephone, that he was "going crazy again." In the same frenetic exchange he told her that at some point in every day of the previous six months he had contemplated killing himself, but he quickly added that he was no longer harboring such thoughts. Then, as later, he must have always realized that suicidal threats would invite hospitalization, and he had vowed that he would never endure that again.

Nevertheless, there were clearly occasions when he believed that his relationship with Vicky had finally enabled him to envisage a joyous "normal" life. One evening we sat together in the living room and he talked with animation about the progress of the romance.

"Maybe there will be a miracle," he said. It was said soberly, without any manic light dancing in his eyes. He talked about the renewed importance of getting a better job so that he would be in a position to support a wife and the two children she would bring with her from her previous marriage. When I indicated that we would be prepared to help them until he was able to take over, he insisted that he wanted to be able to assume the full responsibilities.

So serious and realistic were his words that I began to believe again that he was winning his long battle. Perhaps the combination of Vicky and Dr. Eighth was the wondrous formula we had sought so long. Of course there was a romanticism about the equation, and Nancy was less optimistic; Vicky was still periodically going into the hospital during regressions of her own. Nancy's reservations were fortified too soon by indications of new strains.

One cold, snowy evening in late winter Michael was on the telephone with Vicky for a long time. He emerged angrily. He said that she was "driving me mad" by insisting on maintaining a simultaneous relationship with a young man whom Michael described as a drug addict. I suggested to him that she might be doing this to invite his jealousy and persuade him to propose marriage. He grimly rejected that theory, although acknowledging that he had not been prepared to ask her to marry him. A little while later the phone rang. After a brief conversation Michael came out elatedly and said he was on his way to see Vicky. He called at about 3:00 A.M. to say that he would be late getting back; I suggested that, in view of the weather, it might be wiser for him to remain there overnight and go directly to work. But about two hours later I heard him enter the apartment. I asked him how the evening had gone and he replied laconically, "It was great for a while but I stayed too long. I nearly killed her before I left." He did not elaborate.

Meanwhile he was continuing his sessions with Dr. Eighth. We assumed that she knew what was happening; she was still not disposed to see us, according to Dr. Sixth.

Mike and Vicky's relationship deteriorated. He would say he had decided not to see her again and would not speak to her if she called. Then she would call, and he would visit her and return vowing that he would never see her again. On Tuesday of the week he died—two nights before he took the deadly pills— he had a long, apparently bitter telephone call with her. We never knew what it was about. We did know that she had planned to move into a room in a hotel near our home.

After Michael's death, Vicky came to see us. We spoke quietly together, but we could not bear to press her for any details of their final talk. We told her that we hoped she would continue to visit us. Her own life seemed confused and uncertain; her children were temporarily staying with her parents while she lived alone and held a transient job as a saleswoman. As she walked toward the door she suddenly cried out, "Oh, Michael, why didn't you wait?"

XIV

Warning from a Friend

MICHAEL could see no future in his market research job, and the future of the agency was itself uncertain. In late winter business fell off and some people were let out. While Mike was kept on, it was for fewer hours a week. Meanwhile, he had again begun to make plans to go back to school. He still had no college degree, the clock was running, his job was increasingly precarious and tedious, and the approach of another spring seemed once again to dramatize the years already lost.

The old problems were again in the forefront: Was he ready or able to study? Would the health service at Harvard agree to his readmission? Could he get along at college after all that had intervened? What would he do about the comprehensive exams he had not passed five years before? Should he try to get into a school in New York? Again he began to study catalogues. He submitted an application to New York University, but Harvard was still most on his mind. He started once more to get in touch with the Harvard authorities and to talk frequently about going to summer school.

Late one afternoon in April of that fragile spring, I received a phone call at my office from Phil, a man in his mid-thirties who had been working with Michael at the market research organization for several months. Some weeks earlier Phil had come home with Michael to stay overnight with us after his own basement apartment in the Village had been flooded. Phil was an actor by profession but, like so many others, his theatrical employment was irregular and he had to work elsewhere for supplementary income.

That was the only occasion on which Nancy and I met him; we instinctively liked him. When the three of us became engaged in a rather extended discussion on the market research business, Michael abruptly but politely withdrew and went to bed, as he so often did on such occasions. Phil and I talked until about midnight. He echoed many of the grievances about the sterility and irrelevance of the enterprise that Michael had begun to express some days earlier. But he betrayed less anger about it, no doubt because he viewed it as a convenient auxil-iary to his active theatrical interest. Michael saw it only as an-other personal quagmire. He voiced discomfort about the physi-cal oppressiveness of the office as well as the shallowness of the work; he could not care about which toothpaste fared well in a sampling, or why.

Phil's friendship with Michael and his solicitude about him were apparent and reassuring. They gave us the deceptively re-laxed sense that, with both Phil and Mrs. Ruth Clark, one of the executives of the organization whom we had known for many years, on the scene, Michael was at least surrounded by human warmth that might partially compensate for what he regarded as another demeaning position in life.

Now Phil was on the phone, speaking with mingled concern and hesitancy. He said he had debated at length before calling me, but finally felt an obligation to do so. He said Michael had told him earlier that week that he had spent the previous week-end, while Nancy and I were in Westport, looking for a place to purchase a gun with which to kill himself. Phil implored me not to indicate to Michael that he had spoken to me; I assured him I would respect his admonition. At the same time I said I thought the doctor should know at once; he agreed.

I had no doubt about the authenticity of Phil's account; his reticence and lack of hysteria accentuated the gravity of the alarm. I realized as he was talking that Michael had an appoint-ment at almost that hour with Dr. Eighth, and I did not press Phil for any additional details. What seemed most urgent at that moment was for Dr. Eighth to get the report.

Under the ground rules still operative, I could not communi-cate with her directly. (We had still never met or even spoken by telephone.) I called Dr. Sixth, who came to the phone after I had explained to the woman who answered that I had an emer-gency message for him.

As soon as I had finished recounting Phil's story, Dr. Sixth made clear that he viewed it very seriously. At the same time he agreed that Michael's relationship with Phil should not be jeopardized by any disclosure of the source of the warning. He said he would call Dr. Eighth at once—he knew that she was seeing Michael then or shortly thereafter—and entrust her with the information while emphasizing the importance of "protecting" Phil.

I reached home shortly before Michael returned from his appointment with Dr. Eighth. When he came in, he was distraught and angry. He demanded to know why I had passed on a transparently false story.

"It's Phil who's really sick," he said. "He was talking to me all weekend about how depressed he was."

The realization that Dr. Eighth had so instantly—and incredibly—violated the confidence was shattering. I tried to minimize the debacle by saying that perhaps there had been a misunderstanding but that I had no doubt of Phil's worthy intentions and honest anxiety. Again Michael reiterated that Phil's tale was a fantasy; he went back to his room and closed the door. Then, as so many times before, I debated whether to follow him and had dark imaginings of what he might do in solitude. Again I was restrained by a dread of complicating his psychiatric treatment by some criticism of Dr. Eighth's inexplicable betrayal.

Michael came out of his room after a while. In the interim Dr. Eighth had called him. He seemed calmer and said quietly once more that Phil had invented a story and added almost persuasively that we had no reason to fear that he was contemplating anything like that.

"You don't have to worry about that," he said.

Of course we could not be unworried. As soon as I could, I called Dr. Sixth and told him what had happened. He was startled and dismayed. He said he had stressed to Dr. Eighth that there must be no reference to what Phil had said; he could not conceive of what had impelled her to ignore his words. He said he would call her immediately and try to find out what had gone so terribly wrong.

Later that evening Dr. Sixth called us back. As Nancy and I listened on separate phones (by then Michael had retired for the night), he said he had spoken to Dr. Eighth and was utterly unable to obtain a satisfactory explanation for her disclosure. "I can't understand it," he kept repeating. He could only say that she was not disposed to be apprehensive about what Phil had said and that Michael had promised her that if he ever contemplated suicide, he would talk to her at once. Dr. Sixth agreed that her indiscretion had imperiled Michael's friendship with Phil, which seemed even more urgent now, and had once again placed me in an adversary relationship with Michael. In his view Phil had betrayed him and I was his accomplice.

Now there recurs the question that haunts this chronicle: Why did we let the matter rest there? Why didn't we insist on seeing Drs. Sixth and Eighth at once and try to discover both why she had acted on her own and why she was seemingly unshaken by Phil's report? Why didn't we at least insist that Phil be asked to talk with one or both of them, or all four of us, so that we could resolve any uncertainty about the nature of the message he had given me? Why were we sedated by Dr. Eighth's assurance, transmitted to us by Dr. Sixth, that Michael had promised not to harm himself without consulting her? We knew that he had vowed never to be hospitalized again. How could we have been so deaf to such clear alarms?

There are no good answers. All of us were guilty of an incomprehensible negligence.

A few days later Dr. Sixth, obviously troubled by the episode, called us to say that he had again talked with Dr. Eighth after Michael had visited her again. He said once more that he still could not comprehend why, without consultation with any of us, she had flouted his secrecy stricture. But he said she had now told him that she felt there had been a salutary sequel to the episode; no details were offered but the tone of the remark was that Michael was in better shape. And that seemed to be true, for about two weeks.

I did not speak to Phil again until a few hours after Michael's death. I had called Mrs. Clark to tell her what had happened and to thank her for her effort in his behalf. Then I asked her to let me tell Phil. When I began to break the news he said in anguish, "What are you trying to tell me?" I told him and I apologized for our failure to recognize that he had known more than Michael's doctors or parents. I shall never know whether he was too grieved or too bitter to respond; he turned the phone back silently to Mrs. Clark.

Among Michael's unpublished poems that we found after his death, there appeared these lines, dated March, 1969, and thus apparently written a few weeks before his conversation with Phil:

> So rare that the sun
> Shines in my face
> It's absence from my
> Soul is God's disgrace.
> Maybe one day, when I
> am one, my soul
> will be connected with the sun.

XV

Dr. Seventh's Phone Call

IN THE BEGINNING OF MAY, Mike became more withdrawn, nervous, and hostile than he had been for a long time. He was avoiding the predinner cocktail with Nancy in the living room; instead he would go to his own room and have a drink by himself. Dinner-table conversation (just Nancy and Michael most of the time) was always hard to sustain and had become more filled with long silences. If they had not finished eating when I arrived, Michael would greet me perfunctorily and soon retire to his room. Occasionally he now responded to things in a way reminiscent of earlier moods when a psychotic state was coming on. Until then, ever since the early period at Brightlawn, there had been no such symptoms. Now there was no single episode, only disturbing echoes of past flare-ups. He must have felt himself slipping again into psychosis and seen another hospital looming. He began to talk about Dr. Seventh, whom he had not mentioned for several months. He asked Nancy why she thought Dr. Seventh had never let him listen to the tapes of the sodium amytal sessions.

This chapter was initially written on the evening of Tuesday, May 12, 1970, in the week we had quietly dreaded because it was the anniversary of Michael's last week of life. And it was on Tuesday of that week that another warning was so clearly signaled and sadly unexplored.

That Tuesday afternoon, through one of those coincidences that we must either view as premonitory or bizarre, Dr. Seventh had unexpectedly telephoned me. It had been quite a while since our last meeting and his departure. Nancy and I had occasionally expressed disappointment and even resentment about his silence. As in the long vanishing act of Dr. First, we could not conceal a feeling that an abandonment had occurred once again, and this time perhaps that it was we, along with Michael, who had been deserted.

I welcomed the sound of Seventh's cheerful, animated voice. He explained that he had been obliged to come into the city for a brief visit but was about to leave again. When he inquired about Michael, I was tentative: "It seems to depend on which day of the week it is." Dr. Seventh said he was sorry he could not see us during that trip but we expressed a mutual hope that we could arrange to get together on his next trip to New York. He gave me his unlisted New England telephone number, saying that we should not hesitate to call if we felt he could be helpful.

That evening Michael's demeanor was ominous. After Nancy had retired and I had finished reading proofs, he came into the living room, looking strained and disconsolate. He had been complaining for several days about how insufferable his job was; now there was a new feverishness in his protest. We had agreed in conversations during the previous week that it might be wise for him to look for another job but that it would be foolish for him to quit until he had one. Now this no longer seemed satisfactory. When I pressed the point, he became quite combative and suddenly said, "You know, my doctor tells me I can't get better unless I can express my aggressions."

I remember an emotion of despair, a sense of futile reenactment at this reversion to the Freudian jargon that Dr. Seventh had tried to thrust aside. I also believe Michael must have seen an expression signifying hopelessness and that it must have in some way compounded his own deepening fears about himself. He left the room but returned shortly and said, "You don't have Dr. Seventh's number, do you?"

Instantly and impetuously, I lied. To give him Seventh's long-distance number might provoke a disaffection and distrust in our relations with Dr. Sixth and his protégé Dr. Eighth, who were, after all, now in charge. Nancy, who had overheard the conversation from our bedroom, said she agreed. (Earlier Mike had asked her if she knew how to reach Dr. Seventh, but she had also failed to respond.)

How could we have been so wrong? Dr. Eighth, whom we had never met, had brushed off Phil's warning and even the plea for discretion; yet we were now primarily concerned about her sensibilities, apprehensive that the reemergence of Dr. Seventh might lead to her exit from the scene and perhaps antagonize Dr. Sixth, who had so much faith in her healing powers. The thought of imploring her, and perhaps both of them, not to take offense and to remain assured of our highest esteem, as Dr. First had so often demanded, froze our judgment. We were intimidated and, perhaps worse, drained of energy for another encounter.

No, we do not know what would have happened if I had given Michael Dr. Seventh's phone number. The call might not have gotten through; he might have been harassed and distracted and have suggested that he would see Michael at some future date when he came to New York. But perhaps he might have urged us all to come up for a visit (he had spoken sometime earlier of our doing so during the approaching summer). If we had, we can never know that anything would have been achieved beyond some delaying action; yet perhaps a reinstatement of shock treatment might have been arranged.

What I know is that the reason I lied to Michael is that we had lost confidence in our capacity to intervene in the process of treatment. We had abdicated again.

Sometime before daylight the next morning I was roused by the sound of our dog barking at the closed door of Michael's room. I persuaded him to be quiet. But when I awakened again I had a sudden, haunting thought that the dog had been trying to alert us. Nancy had already left for work. I rushed into Michael's room and saw his empty bed. Then—blessedly—I heard his voice on the telephone in Holly's bedroom. When I went in he was neatly dressed and combed; he hung up when he saw me and said he had been talking to a faculty member at Harvard about his plans for returning to college. He also said he had called his office to explain that he would be a little late. He seemed calm and undisturbed, in contrast to the evening before.

Soon thereafter he left for work. I felt rather relieved that I had decided not to give him Dr. Seventh's number and thereby introduced some unpredictable complexities into the current therapeutic situation. Although I was concerned about Michael's

reference to the necessity for airing his aggressions—because it
seemed a revival of the language of the Dr. First period—it
seemed most important to avoid another break in the continuity.
I toyed with the idea of calling Dr. Sixth or Dr. Eighth myself
and reporting what had occurred. But I didn't. I still feared that
the reentry of Dr. Seventh might "complicate" things and perhaps even cost us the services of Dr. Eighth.

XVI

"One Has the Choice ..."

Apr 2? '69
One has the choice to live or die.
One has the choice to fall or fly.
But how can I make myself choose
My death?
How can I
Sometimes one can choose the
Anger, and then not need to cry.
But wanting to die, yet unable
to choose to; and knowing that
A man should not.
[Poem found among Michael's papers]

AT THE START of the second week of May, Dr. Eighth had begun having longer sessions with Michael. Apprehensive as we were about the signs that he might be losing control, we were reassured by her move (although we might have remembered that exactly the same stepped-up program was followed by Dr. Third before the suicidal "gesture" in 1964).

On May 15 he had one of those unusually protracted sessions. Dr. Eighth was to tell us the next day that it had been largely devoted to talking about his plans for going back to Harvard; she had not found any cause for alarm. (But fellow workers at the office later told us that he had been conspicuously agitated that day.) When he came home for supper, which he had alone with Nancy, he was late, which was rare. She found him tense and gloomy, and it was almost impossible to sustain any conversation. Immediately afterward he said he was going out "to get something" and came back soon carrying a package of cigars. We have never ascertained whether he simultaneously filled a prescription for drugs. But when Nancy looked through his desk the next day, several hours after he had been pronounced dead, she found a drawer full of empty drug bottles that had been prescribed by different doctors. One large bottle was dated May 15.

It was a few minutes before eight when I reached home. Late that afternoon the Associated Press ticker had carried a story describing the growing affluence of market research organizations. In view of Michael's restiveness about his job, I had the trivial hope that he would be encouraged by the news. He had so often indicated a yearning for financial independence—and even dreamed so many wild schemes of quick success—that I thought this progress report might give him momentary pleasure, or at least reconciliation to what he had been describing as insufferable drudgery.

He was seated in his large chair when I entered the room; his face was rather flushed, and his expression was that blend of anger and misery I had seen too often. Nevertheless I handed him the wire copy and made some hearty remark about his fortunate association with a flourishing industry. He glanced irritably at the report and almost shouted, "I couldn't give less of a goddamn about this business."

I retreated at once and closed his door as I left. How often it had happened this way and how often had he construed my reluctance to press an invasion of his privacy, or my incapacity to endure further rebuff, as a sign of disinterest or aloofness? Basically this indicated my unwillingness or incapacity to treat him as if he were acutely ill; if he had complained of a stomachache or some equivalent discomfort, I would have been quick to recommend remedies. But I had really lost any ability to explore the troubled matters of his mind. Dr. Seventh had told us so many times, in Michael's presence, that it was up to Michael to decide whether he wanted to live. He had admonished us not to deal with him as if he were an ailing child.

Moreover, I knew that in later afternoon of that day Michael had kept his appointment with Dr. Eighth. While it was apparent that it had not produced any calm, I could not help recalling what he had said two nights earlier—that she had told him of his need to articulate his aggressions. His demeanor seemed consistent with that counsel.

So Nancy and I, as we sat in the living room and talked about this "regression" while Michael remained in solitude behind his closed door, had no terrifying sense about his mood.

Then, a little after eleven o'clock, Michael came out of his room. He said he was very tired and was going to sleep (this was often how he said good night). He appeared weary but much more relaxed. In a familiar gesture he waved to us, and there was that faint, gentle smile that seemed to survive all the inner pain of so many years.

A moment or two later, he reappeared and said again that he wanted to get to sleep and added, "If anyone calls me, don't wake me up."

I asked, "Are you expecting a call?" We assumed he was trying to avoid another conversation with Vicky.

"No," he replied, "not really."

His voice was even, subdued, almost tranquil. We were never to hear it again.

It is still very hard to write of the morning on which we found Michael and of the rest of that day.

Nancy arose somewhat later than usual. By the time she was ready to leave—it was almost 8:45—Michael should have finished his solitary breakfast and been preparing to leave for his job. When Nancy realized he had not appeared, we discussed whether to awaken him. I urged her to do so, without confessing any of the anxiety I had felt on the previous morning. A few seconds after she entered his room she was calling to me from his bedroom:

"I don't like the way Michael looks."

I jumped out of bed with a sickening dread, and yet, I must add, a stubborn disbelief in any finality. Michael had been so close to death before; thank heaven, I thought, that we had agreed to interrupt his sleep.

But not nearly soon enough.

After we had vainly tried for a few minutes to rouse him by shaking him, applying cold towels, verbally imploring him to awaken, Nancy went to the telephone in the foyer to call the police emergency number (911), which we had both probably mentally rehearsed many times before. While she did so, I telephoned Dr. Arthur Seligman, our physician, who remained on the line. He immediately instructed me to tell Nancy to feel Michael's pulse; after thirty or forty seconds she was crying out, "I can't feel any pulse."

Very swiftly Patrolmen James O'Sullivan and William Young appeared. When they did, Dr. Seligman admonished me to tell them "time is crucial." Then one of them, who had looked at Michael, took the phone, and from the tone of his words it was obvious that he considered things extremely grim if not hopeless. And this was plainly not his first case.

It took about fifteen minutes for the ambulance to arrive. Throughout those endless moments Nancy, under the direction of the police, desperately tried mouth-to-mouth resuscitation. At several points one of the policemen telephoned to underline the urgency of ambulance service; the other feverishly and grimly massaged Michael's chest while Nancy continued to try to breathe life into him.

Later Nancy was to say that both men labored "as if Michael was their own son" and I wrote gratefully of "the police officers whom he had never met" who dedicated themselves to his rescue.

At last the ambulance arrived and Michael was carried on a stretcher into the elevator. When we reached the street they told us there would be room only for Nancy in the vehicle en route to the hospital a little less than a mile away.

There were no empty cabs in sight so I began running from the corner of Eightieth Street and West End Avenue to the nearby subway station at Seventy-ninth Street and Broadway. But about half a block from the station I saw a police patrol car and frantically halted it. When I asked the driver for a hitch to Roosevelt Hospital, he began explaining that the locale was beyond his area of operation. But when I plaintively described the urgency of the situation, he relented. I never did learn his name.

By the time we reached the hospital Michael had been rushed into the emergency area. Nancy was in the crowded waiting room and we were both taken shortly thereafter to a more private refuge across the hall from where the last effort to salvage Michael's life was taking place.

We were incapable of speech; at least neither of us can re-

call saying anything. I remember thinking that, if Michael survived, he again faced hospital "imprisonment"; yet I knew how
desperately, perhaps selfishly, I hoped the miracle of Massachusetts General, where he had been taken after his motor-bike accident, would be repeated. Then—was it fifteen or twenty minutes later?—the young doctor came out. He was smiling
vaguely, and I looked at Nancy with a wild hope. When he said
nothing at once, I found myself asking, "Is there any life?"

I had misread the smile—it was the nervous manifestation of
a youthful physician still not hardened to such encounters.

"No, he must have been dead for several hours when you
found him," he said softly. He asked us whether we wanted any
pills. We numbly shook our heads.

From that awful instant we had obviously made a mutual, silent vow to stand up and think about Holly, to whom we would
have to break the news as well as to Nancy's parents, both of
them so deeply devoted to Michael and vulnerable to shock.
One of the policemen, who had lingered for the result, gallantly
found a cab for us.

We did not want Holly to be alone when she heard the news
and so there ensued a frustrating interlude while we tried to locate David. Finally we found them together; David responded
with a cry of pain and, by the time Holly came to the phone,
she knew that there would be no uncertainty to be described.

I reminded her that we had talked in the past of the possibility of Michael's suicide, particularly after the window episode in
our apartment, and she had extracted a pledge, with a mixture
of grimness and feigned frivolity, that I would not "have a heart
attack." (She had greater confidence in Nancy's fortitude than in
mine.) I recalled that conversation to her and said I had kept
my pledge and hoped she would reciprocate by trying to absorb
the blow. Then and thereafter she and David were magnificent,
as were so many others. My brother quickly agreed to serve as
my stand-in for the identification of the body; it is one of the
larger idiocies of the Medical Examiner's office that this could
not take place at the hospital and a special ceremony was required at the morgue.

In deference to Nancy's quick, quiet statement the moment
we returned home that "we've got to keep doing things," we
completed the notifications. During one interlude Nancy's eyes

clouded with tears. I said something like "We did everything we could do." She said, "No, we didn't." Of course she was right.

Then, in early afternoon, Dr. Eighth called. (Dr. Seligman had volunteered to tell her what had happened when I spoke to him from the hospital.) I answered the phone and she began almost at once, after an expression of sorrow, to insist that Michael's death must have been the result of an accidental misuse of various medications; it was imperative, she said, that we make immediate arrangements for an autopsy.

I found myself barely listening and trying to avoid some bitter exclamation. Michael was dead, beyond any redemption by autopsy. Her medical inquisitiveness could not have seemed less consequential at that moment, no matter how sympathetic. Then, almost mercifully, I heard Nancy saying, "I've found Michael's note." As she walked out of his room, I told Dr. Eighth of the discovery that rendered our discussion pointless. There was a terrible pause. Then she asked if we would like her to visit us and I said I thought it would be better to postpone a meeting until a later time.

What was there to say? It had all ended in a caricature of the beginning. I was talking to a doctor whom Nancy and I had never met, just as Michael had started his therapy nearly ten years earlier with a doctor similarly unknown to us, who had refused to grant us an interview until a time of his own choosing. Dr. Eighth had discounted Phil's alert; she had seen Michael for a long time during the late afternoon of his final day and detected nothing that inspired any fear. Until Michael's note was found, she had convinced herself—and was attempting to persuade me—that his death must have been a pharmaceutical accident.

Later she wrote us a note recapitulating their last conversation. In it she described how he was quite earnest in discussing his desire to return to Harvard. She volunteered the broader assessment that he had suffered from a very deep sickness. But that was not what she was saying at the moment when Nancy found the note.

Like all the others, she had tried and failed. What could be gained from psychiatric reminiscence and mutual consolation?

The only endurable thought was that Michael was free at last.

XVII

Postscript

Now it is July, 1971, nearly twenty-six months since Michael's death, as these concluding words are written in Westport, where, we like to believe, Michael spent many joyful summers from 1949 until the onset, or overt manifestation, of illness more than a decade later.

As Nancy and I reread the preceding pages—pieced together during vacation and odd hours of many nights and weekends, even small passages debated, reexamined, and revised before finally set down—there remains an uneasiness about whether we have, in certain places, said too little and, in others, more than was warranted by our knowledge.

Having disclaimed any intention to write what could be considered a biography of Michael, rather than essentially the history of his sickness and the quest for relief, we are sadly aware that the portrait of him is too often one-dimensional. Even the excerpts from his own writings are drawn primarily from intervals when he was either in mental hospitals or on drugs; they can offer only a glimpse of creative gifts, on so many levels that were unrealized. Nor have I adequately recorded the capacity for the enjoyment of life and zestful companionship that characterized his earlier years and that, even in some dreary times of hospitalization, would light up anew, if only for brief moments. (When he left Grace Hills, his fellow patients presented him with a testimonial headed "We'll Miss You.")

In much of this chronicle he appears aloof, abstracted, even surly. Not enough of it describes the solicitude he so often extended to his parents, his sister, and others, his remorse over what he deemed his burdensome predicament, his rage over his inability to overcome the disease that tormented him, and, above all, the quiet graciousness he tried to sustain when he was plagued by the dread of regression. Indeed, I have often thought that it was an excessive regard for the dignity he tried to maintain that made us ineffectual, and seemingly insensitive, when we should have heard and seen the distress signals and responded with greater concern and love.

But these misgivings relate not only to the incompleteness of the portrait of Michael. This has been primarily an account of our bewilderment, confusion, and despair as his illness evolved. Yet it does not define with any precision the illness or explain its cause or confidently point the way to some obvious "cure" we missed along the way.

We are no wiser now than before about whether Michael's affliction, in the present state of medical knowledge, was hopeless or whether he was ultimately a victim of a fatal blindness on the part of parents and therapists alike. One psychiatrist whom we respect told us afterward that suicide occurred most frequently among patients "just when they had begun to get better," but this only confirms our sense that the final warning we received from Phil was inexcusably minimized by both ourselves and the two therapists to whom it was transmitted.

On the other hand, Nancy recalls Dr. Seventh saying in 1968, when Michael's last hospitalization was about to end, "I wish I had gotten hold of Mike a few years earlier." He was most mistrustful of orthodox private treatment, and seems to have succeeded in other cases with a practical combination of family therapy and insulin.

In describing the absurd, abysmal failures of communication that marred our relationships with most of the therapists we encountered, we may seem to be saying that all would have been well if the air had been clear. But it was not they, of course, who created Michael's illness, nor do I suggest that they have not served others far better than they did Michael. They might respond, as Dr. First did on occasion, that our failures as parents aggravated, if they did not cause, the problem. Certainly it is true that Michael had the misfortune to have parents preoccupied with the turbulence of their own careers, and a father so deeply engrossed with saving the world, at cocktail parties as well as on other fronts, that he must have been oblivious for far too long to the troubled eyes of his son.

It is also a matter for conjecture how much genetic factors or chemical imbalance may have contributed to Michael's condition. It was Dr. Liss who first talked about the chemical question; only Dr. Seventh of all of Michael's therapists took it seriously.

But whatever *mea culpas* I may feel obliged to offer for belated recognition of Michael's problems, there still seems no semblance of rationality in the inhibitions initially imposed by Dr. First and tragically resurrected by Dr. Eighth on parental inquiry and involvement.

Obviously we do not *know* that anything would have been different if Dr. First had been a different man operating under a different set of rules. Yet we cannot avoid asking ourselves whether the course of events might not have been altered if, as at least some therapists now believe, we had not been excluded from participation in the treatment. Dr. Seventh, for example, strongly felt that only therapy linking parents and children could work in cases such as Michael's. He once likened the three of us to rubber bands—tension on any had to affect the others; Michael could not go it alone.

Meanwhile, Michael was subjected to a long series of conflicting theories and techniques over too many years. Sometimes, as in the Thorazine treatment at Statewide, he was required to defraud the doctors in trying to save himself from becoming a "vegetable." By the time he had reached Dr. Eighth, he was once again being subjected to the Freudian rituals that Dr. Seventh had so plainly, and with at least temporary success, ruled out as a futile round of reverie and recrimination. And when we learned this was happening, we did not ask any questions; we did not even insist upon talking about it with the doctor, anymore than we had questioned her disparagement of the significance of Phil's phone call.

It is nearly midnight; I look out the window and imagine young Michael returning home after a Westport party, his face animated, his eyes alive and unhaunted. He may even pause to tell me sympathetically of some foolish character who disgraced himself during the evening. He is at once handsome, diffident, relaxed, and soon to begin his senior year in high school. It will not occur to me to ask whether anything is troubling him.

Now there is so much we will never really know.

DATE DUE

APR 2 7 2004			

Demco, Inc. 38-293